BIG BOOK of Behavior Boosters

150 Fun & Simple Ideas that Motivate Positive Behavior

Ashley K. Goertemiller

Copyright © 2011 by Ashley K. Goertemiller

BIG BOOK *of Behavior Boosters*
by Ashley K. Goertemiller

Printed in the United States of America

ISBN 9781619040403

All rights reserved solely by the author. The author guarantees all contents are original and do not infringe upon the legal rights of any other person or work. Except as permitted under the United States Copyright Act, no part of this book may be reproduced or distributed in any form or by any means, without prior written permission from the author. The only exception to this prohibition is a one-time copy allowance for personal use. Send all inquiries to customerservice@behaviorboosters.com. The views expressed in this book are not necessarily those of the publisher.

Unless otherwise indicated, Bible quotations are taken from THE HOLY BIBLE, ENGLISH STANDARD VERSION (ESV), Copyright© 2001 by Crossway Bibles and THE HOLY BIBLE, NEW INTERNATIONAL VERSION (NIV)®, Copyright© 2011 by Biblica, Inc.™

www.xulonpress.com

What people are saying...

These applicable ideas make it easy for me and my wife to be more positive with our children. –Dean, SC

As a teacher I love material like this. I've found something that improves behavior and focuses on the positive. –Kim, NY

Having the ideas laid out instead of just another book to read makes positive parenting go from "someday" to "today". –Elizabeth, NC

These books are great! We can work on teaching our children Scripture in positive ways that mean something to them. You bridge the gap between the infant-training stage and the teach-them-theology stage. –Pastor Troy, MN

My kids are having a great time finding ways to be positive with one another and I feel confident that this is something I can do with my kids and not just leave it up to my wife. Thank you. –Tony, NC

We purchased the books out of curiosity and are so glad! The kids are having a blast with the different Boosters, and we love how they're learning to apply Scripture in such meaningful ways. –Steve & Liz, GA

I was skeptical at first, but the ideas are so simple and fun and helped me see that we can do this as a family! – Sandy, KY

I didn't grow up in a positive environment but want to be encouraging and positive with my children. Your book makes it easy. –father, GA

These ideas are awesome! It already has made such a difference in the tone of our household! –Cherie, NC

I use Behavior Boosters with my kids and love the results! –Tam, TN

You've given me great tools as I raise my children to follow God. I look forward to using these ideas with my little ones, and the preschoolers at church. –Dana, GA

You put into words the steps and guidelines that will assist parents in their most important job! –Grandma Ann, TN

A Word from the Author

Thank you for choosing Behavior Boosters among hundreds, if not thousands, of positive parenting books. I hope you and your child(ren) will enjoy using the ideas in this book as much as I've enjoyed creating them!

This book came into fruition from a simple prayer of wanting Scripture to be meaningful to my children, and that they would behave out of their own heart's desire; not because of the disciplinary actions that would take place if they didn't.

After jotting down simple ideas to emphasize various Scriptures, trying the Boosters out on my kids, and sharing them with family and friends, the ideas caught on. Adults and children alike enjoyed them and asked for more. Upon receiving encouragement from others who were using the Boosters in their households, I decided to make Behavior Boosters "official". What an exciting, humbling, and unexpected journey this has been!

I pray that Behavior Boosters will be a continual blessing to your family as you strive to serve the Lord with the child(ren) He has given you.

Extending…

Sincere thanks to my patient parents, supportive siblings, and faithful friends for helping brainstorm and edit, and for allowing me to expand upon your ideas.
What creative minds you have!

Deep thanks to my handsome husband, whose tenderness calms me, passion awes me, friendship warms me, wisdom grows me, and quick wit humors me. I love you, Kevin.
What wife could want more!

Special thanks to my sweet children for being enthusiastic test models with each new idea. You truly are the best kids a mom could have and so much more than your mom deserves.
What treasures I've been blessed with!

Utmost thanks to my Lord & Savior who forgives my constant failings without hesitation, and continually guides me to hide His Word in my heart and impress it upon the hearts and minds of my children (Deuteronomy 11:18-19).
What grace has been given to me!

How to Use Behavior Boosters

This book is designed as an easy reference of ideas to boost specific behaviors with your child(ren) while teaching them applicable Scripture. My goal in writing this book is to provide you with a variety of fun, yet simple "Boosters" that will motivate you to continually encourage your children in their Godly character development.

The books are printed in black & white for ease of copying and so that your children can color the pages. The Boosters are also printable straight from your computer at *BehaviorBoosters.com*. While visiting the website, find out more about speaking engagements, free downloadables, and other books and materials that are available (and don't forget to pass along your findings to a friend!).

My hope and prayer is that you and your children will apply these Bible verses to your life every single day therefore deeply rooting God's Word into your hearts so that the desire to honor Him becomes an automatic response.

Please contact customerservice@behaviorboosters.com with any questions or suggestions. Enjoy!!

Topical Index
Title

A"maize"ing Grace	attitude
aCROSStic	attitude
Advent-ures	Scripture application
Ants in My Pants	self-initiative
Arky, Arky	cooperation
Attitude Adjustors	attitude/Scripture application
Be the 1	thankfulness
Bee Attitudes	Scripture application
Behavior Beans	behavior
Behavior Bucks	behavior
Bless You Box	thankfulness
Bloomin' Onion	confidence
Boldness Baldy	confidence
Bountiful Blessings	thankfulness
Building Blocks	encouragement
Butterfly Kisses	kindness/love
Button Basket	tone of voice/self-control
Call Me	prayer
Caring Caterpillar	kindness/caring
Caring Clover	kindness/caring
Catch Praise	encouragement
Caterpillar Countdown	behavior
Cheery O's	joyfulness
Chocolate Lovers	love
Chore Champ	responsibility
Clean Heart	attitude
Color by Number	wise choices
Complaint Can	peace
Cookie Jar	behavior
Cookie Press	behavior
Cooperation Coordinates	cooperation
Cross Stitch	behavior
Crown Him with Many Crayons	attitude
Delite Bright	honesty
Doer Daisy	self-initiative/thoughtfulness
Do-Unto's	self-control/peace
Dream Weaver	peace

Dress-a-Bear	Scripture application
Eggs-actly!	obedience
Encouragement Elephant	encouragement
Faithful "Fall"ower	wise choices
Fearless Freddy	Scripture application/confidence
Fill 'er Up	joyfulness
Fisher of Men	wise choices
Fix-It Shop	forgiveness
Flower Power	prayer
Friends Fries	prayer
Friendship Fish	kindness
Fruit of the Spirit Tree	Scripture application
Frustration Station	peace
Get Up!	self-initiative
Glad-Libs	joyfulness
God Rocks!	thankfulness/attitude
God's Handy-work	behavior
God's Team	behavior
Grate-fullness	thankfulness
Grow Up	behavior
GRRRattitude	thankfulness/attitude
Hairy Helper	helpfulness
Hamburger Helper	helpfulness
Happiness Hippo	joyfulness
Har-money	cooperation
Heart of Wisdom	wise choices
Heavenly Pair-a-Dice	behavior
Helping Hippo	helpfulness
Hide & Seek-Ye-First	attitude
Hmmm…Interesting	thoughtfulness
Home Sweet Home	Scripture application
Honey, Honey	kindness
Hot Stuff	obedience
Humble Pie	humility
I Am Cape-Able	confidence
I Refuze	peer pressure
In Today's News…	encouragement
J-O-Y Full	joyfulness
Joyful Jumping Jack	joyfulness
Keep me in Stitches	joyfulness
Kinder Reminder	kindness/love

Knight in Shining Armor	Scripture application
Last Place	thoughtfulness/patience
Listening *Lips*	patience
Love Links	love / Scripture application
Love One AnUdder	love
Love Reporter	love
M&M's	thoughtfulness
Maker's Doesen	self-initiative/thoughtfulness
Manner Marks	respect
Map Quest	behavior
Marbleous Jar	behavior
Master Blaster	behavior
Money Talks	tone of voice/kindness
Mouth Trap	attitude/tone of voice
Muscle Man	behavior
Music Machine	joyfulness
No Whine Vine, The	tone of voice/attitude
Opossum Opposites	behavior
Ought-to-Dot	wise choices
Patient Prince(ss)	patience
Pearly Gates	wise choices
Penny for Your Talks	tone of voice
Picture Prayers	prayer
Popcorn Praise	prayer
Power of Love	love
Pure Nonsense	Scripture application
Put a Cork in It	honesty
Puzzle Peace	peace
Quick Sand	patience
Rainbow of _____	behavior
Red Hot Obedience Pot	obedience
Red Light, Green Light	behavior
Respecter Gadget	respect/obedience
Responsibility Chart	responsibility
Ruler of All	obedience
Salt & Light	thoughtfulness
See Creatures	self-initiative/helpfulness
Self-Control Remote	self-control/peace
Share Bear	thoughtfulness
Sibling Revelry	cooperation/encouragement
Sign Me Up	behavior

Smack!	honesty
Smartie Pants	behavior
Sneakers	honesty
Son Dial	attitude
Sondae	peer pressure
Sonflower	self-initiative/thoughtfulness
Sow What?	peace/cooperation
Specktacles	responsibility
Step Right Up	behavior
Strike a Pose	attitude
Sweet & Sour Children	attitude
Sweet Treat	behavior
Taste Bud-dy	tone of voice/attitude
Tattle Tail	peace
Ten Commandments Train	obedience
Terrific Tickets	behavior
That's Twisted!	cooperation
This Little Light of Mine	attitude
Truth Time	honesty
Truthful Tortoise	honesty
V-I-C-T-O-R-Y	joyfulness
Waves of Mercy	attitude
Whale of a Lesson, A	Scripture application
Wheel of Blessings	behavior
Why Knot?	obedience
Wisdom Rock	wise choices
Wise as an Owl	humility
X-Ray Vision	attitude
Yes I Can! Can	confidence/attitude
Yield	obedience
Zip It	tone of voice

Although listed alphabetically, in order to be resource efficient, the Boosters in this book may not be in exact order.

A"maize"ing Grace

"For it is by grace you have been saved, through faith."
Ephesians 2:8a

- **Goal**: attitude (demonstrate grace)
- **Preparation Time**: 0-5 minutes
- **Materials Needed**: copy of following page, popcorn (or kernels), glue
- **How to Use**: Each time child demonstrates grace (politeness, generosity, tolerance, forgiveness, etc.) glue a kernel or piece of popcorn onto the corn until full.
- **Additional Ideas**: Write an example of grace on each row of corn and glue a kernel in a square each time child exhibits that characteristic of grace.
- **Hint**: if using kernels, use thick paper or draw corn onto cardboard since kernels will get heavy
- **Educational Benefit**: vocabulary (grace, maize)
- **Optional Incentive**: enjoy some popcorn together

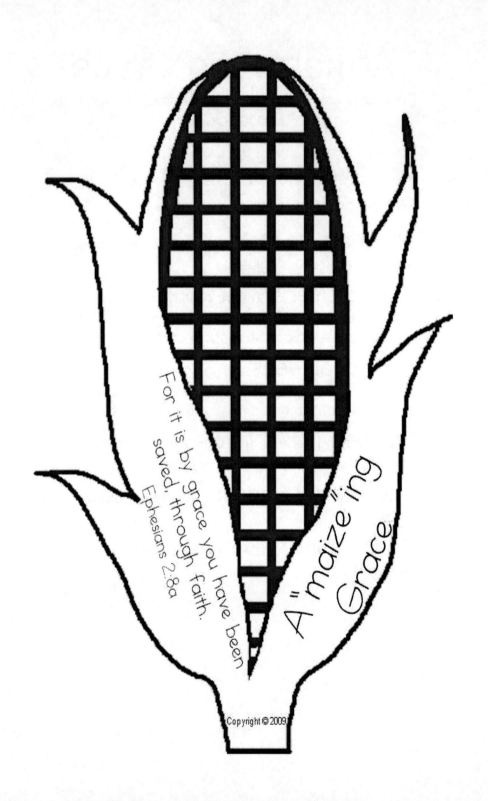

aCROSStic

"Set your minds on things above, not on earthly things."
Colossians 3:2

- **Goal**: attitude (Godly traits)
- **Preparation Time**: 10-15 minutes
- **Materials Needed**: square cut-outs (equal to number of letters in child's name +2) or paper cut into large cross shape, marker
- **How to Use**: Write one letter of child's name on each square (going down). Each day, think of a word for one of the letters that focuses on Jesus and work on achieving that word. aCROSStic is complete when all letters have been used (*e.g. JOEL: J=Joyful, O=Obedient, E=encouraging, L=loving*).
- **Additional Ideas**: have one goal behavior and add a letter of child's name downward each time child demonstrates until cross is complete
- **Hint**: cut paper in thirds lengthwise, tape two strips together at short side, cut third strip in half, and tape on either side of long strip to from a cross shape
- **Educational Benefit**: acrostics, letter recognition
- **Optional Incentive**: have some fun with play-dough using cross cookie cutters or knife to form cross

Advent-ures
Based on Luke 2

- **Goal**: Scripture application (Jesus' birth)
- **Preparation Time**: 0-5 minutes
- **Materials Needed**: Advent calendar (find at a Christian bookstore or internet)
- **How to Use**: Starting on December 1 and each day thereafter, hide the Advent calendar. As a family, go on an "Advent-ure" to find the hidden calendar, then discuss that days' Scripture and the life-changing adventure that happened in Jerusalem so long ago.
- **Additional Ideas**: take turns hiding the calendar and giving clues to its whereabouts
- **Hint**: use in December, before Christmas
- **Educational Benefit**: listening to clues, visual awareness, imagination
- **Optional Incentive**: eat some candy canes and read about the candy's origin (my favorite is <u>The Legend of the Candy Cane</u> by Lori Walburg)

Ants in My Pants

"Go to the ant, you sluggard;
consider its ways and be wise!"
Proverbs 6:6

- **Goal**: self-initiative
- **Preparation Time**: 5-10 minutes
- **Materials Needed**: empty cereal box, scissors, washable stamp pad (black or red), black fine-tip marker
- **How to Use**: Cut apart a cereal box to look like pants. Each time self-motivation is demonstrated, have child press finger onto stamp pad, then onto the pants to form an ant body. Draw antennas and legs onto ant body.
- **Additional Ideas**: Print out several ant pictures and cut apart. Write self-motivation ideas on the ants and when child does one of them without being reminded, glue that ant onto the pants.
- **Hint**: use old fabric scraps to decorate pants with "patches" and/or purchase little plastic ants at a party store to glue on
- **Educational Benefit**: science (ant anatomy), art (fingerprinting)
- **Optional Incentive**: play Ants in the Pants game by Hasbro or purchase an ant farm to observe

Arky, Arky

"Two are better than one because they have
a good return for their labor."
Ecclesiastes 4:9

- **Goal**: cooperation
- **Preparation Time**: 5-10 minutes
- **Materials Needed**: ark (large boat) cut out of cardboard, variety of animal stickers (2 of each animal)
- **How to Use**: When children show cooperation or are working together nicely, choose matching animal stickers to place side-by-side on the ark. Goal is to fill the boat with all pairs of animals as predetermined.
- **Additional Ideas**: For individual child, put one of each animal sticker on the ark. When an example of cooperation is shown, give child a sticker of the matching animal to place next to partner until all the animals are paired.
- **Hint**: use a Noah's Ark toy and place matching plastic animals in boat when cooperation is demonstrated
- **Educational Benefit**: matching pairs
- **Optional Incentive**: go to a zoo and be aware of all the animals (and smells and food) that had to fit on the ark

Attitude Adjustors

"Finally, all of you, live in harmony with one another; be sympathetic, love as brothers, be compassionate and humble. Do not repay evil with evil or insult with insult, but with blessing…"
1 Peter 3:8-9

- **Goal**: attitude / Scripture application
- **Preparation Time**: 0-5 minutes
- **Materials Needed**: craft sticks, jar or baggie
- **How to Use**: Each time child demonstrates a good attitude (characteristic from above), add a craft stick to jar. At the end of the day or week, allow child to "buy" something with craft sticks (optional--see Hint).
- **Additional Ideas**: write Biblical characteristics on each craft stick and give to child when appropriately demonstrated
- **Hint**: Craft sticks may used to "buy" computer time, a later bedtime, game with parent, extra time outside, etc. Doesn't need to be something tangible.
- **Educational Benefit**: counting
- **Optional Incentive**: see Hint

Behavior Beans

"Blessed...are those who hear
the word of God and obey it."
Luke 11:28

- **Goal**: behavior
- **Preparation Time**: 0-5 minutes
- **Materials Needed**: small jar, jelly beans or dry variety
- **How to Use**: *dry beans*--Each time child is behaving well, place a bean in the jar and/or remove bean when child is misbehaving. When jar is filled, goal is reached.
  jelly beans--Fill jar with beans. Each time desired behavior is demonstrated, child may eat one jelly bean.
- **Additional Ideas**: use for schoolwork, teamwork, chores, sportsmanship, etc.
- **Hint**: a small baby food jar takes many beans to fill (pinto@100, lima@40, jelly@65), so this is a long-term accomplishment
- **Educational Benefit**: counting, estimating
- **Optional Incentive**: let child choose special "date" with parent

Be the 1

Read Luke 17:11-19 about the ten men healed of leprosy, then be the one who remembers to be thankful.

- **Goal**: thankfulness
- **Preparation Time**: 0-5 minutes
- **Materials Needed**: copy of following page, scissors, sticky tac
- **How to Use**: Cut out both 1's. Cut the black one into 10 pieces and attach each piece with sticky tac onto the white one to cover it up. Each time child shows thankfulness, remove a "leprous" piece until the thankful 1 remains.
- **Additional Ideas**: Use for any behavior, or general behavior by covering/removing spots each time child demonstrates choosing God above other things.
- **Hint**: Cut out a large number 1 out of an old cereal box. Each time child shows thankfulness, write it on a sticky note and post on the number until the 1 is covered with thankfulness.
- **Educational Benefit**: number recognition, subtraction of parts
- **Optional Incentive**: choose something from the $1 menu at a fast food restaurant

Be the 1 who is thankful.

Bee Attitudes
Matthew 5:3-11

- **Goal**: Scripture application (The Beatitudes*)
- **Preparation Time**: 10-15 minutes
- **Materials Needed**: copy of following page (have child decorate hive and color bees), scissors, writing utensil
- **How to Use**: Write a Beatitude on each line of the hive. As child models a Beatitude, put a bee on the appropriate line of the hive. Goal is achieved when bees are on all sections of the hive.
- **Additional Ideas**: For multiple children, write a Beatitude on each bee and each child's name on the lines of the hive and place the "bee attitude" next to the child's name who demonstrated it.
- **Hint**: *This Booster is intended for older children. The Beatitudes were written for believers, so some of them may be hard concepts for younger children to understand. Please be sure to talk through each one with your children before beginning.
- **Educational Benefit**: Did you know that a bee's body is too heavy for it's wing size? Yet the bees don't complain (if they did, we would have limited honey and pollination) and they have such a good, hard-working attitude.
- **Optional Incentive**: enjoy some honeycomb cereal or make biscuits to eat with honey

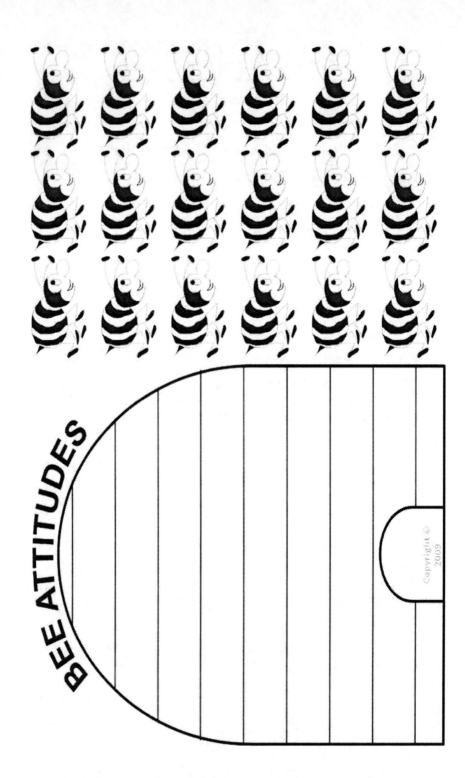

Behavior Bucks

"Make sure that nobody pays back wrong for wrong, but always strive to do what is good for each other and for everyone else."
1 Thessalonians 5:15

- **Goal**: behavior
- **Preparation Time**: 5-10 minutes (initially)
- **Materials Needed**: carnival-style tickets
- **How to Use**: Set goals (1-2 goals x age) with child. Give 5 tickets at the beginning of each week, regardless of how many child has from previous weeks. When behaving, give ticket. When not behaving, take ticket away. At week's end, child may "buy" pre-purchased items from your "store" (candy, $ store items, doll, jewelry, train, eating out, etc.). Reuse tickets, or as child "spends" them, write good behavior on the back and review them at the beginning of the next week.
- **Additional Ideas**: When child leaves out items or is arguing over them, place in "toy jail". If child needs items immediately (shoes, school book, etc.), charge two tickets. If child can wait, items must be bought out of jail before they can shop. If there are unwanted items, donate them.
- **Hint**: appropriate age is 4 years and up
- **Educational Benefit**: earning, spending, saving
- **Optional Incentive**: see "How to Use"

Bless You Box

"…the Lord Jesus himself said:
'It is more blessed to give than to receive'."
Acts 20:35b

- **Goal**: thankfulness
- **Preparation Time**: 5-10 minutes
- **Materials Needed**: empty tissue box, wrapping paper, scissors, tape, marker, small note paper
- **How to Use**: Wrap empty tissue box and entitle "Bless You Box". Fill with blessings you've received (e.g. *My sister hugged me, I got a letter from Grandma, etc.*). Pull out and read when child is feeling discouraged.
- **Additional Ideas**: have child(ren) think of at least one blessing each day and put in box before bed, then review weekly
- **Hint**: encourage children to write the blessings on their own to solidify their thoughts
- **Educational Benefit**: spelling, writing, reading sentences
- **Optional Incentive**: visit a nursing home, have some children over to play so their parents can go out (let child think of a special way to bless others)

Bloomin' Onion

"Blessed is the one who trusts in the Lord,
whose confidence is in him."
Jeremiah 17:7

- **Goal**: confidence
- **Preparation Time**: 5-10 minutes
- **Materials Needed**: small styrofoam ball, pipe cleaners (amount depends on size of ball), permanent marker, masking tape (optional)
- **How to Use**: Write above Scripture around the ball (on masking tape if helpful). Insert pipe cleaners into the bottom, then curve each one around to cover the ball and poke into the top. Each time confidence in demonstrated, have child "peel" one pipe cleaner from the ball.
- **Additional Ideas**: have several types of fruit that have peels available (e.g. oranges, bananas) and let child peel the fruit (to eat or to help make fruit salad for dinner) each time confidence is demonstrated
- **Hint**: pipe cleaners may need to be trimmed down depending on ball size
- **Educational Benefit**: shapes, fine motor skills
- **Optional Incentive**: have dinner at Outback Steakhouse and enjoy a real Bloomin' Onion

Boldness Baldy

"Whatever you do, do it all for the glory of God."
1 Corinthians 10:31b

- **Goal**: confidence
- **Preparation Time**: 5-10 minutes
- **Materials Needed**: small Styrofoam sphere, pipe cleaners (cut into ½" - 1" sections), materials to create face
- **How to Use**: Create face on Styrofoam sphere. Push pipe cleaners into the top as hair. Each time child demonstrates boldness (standing up for what's right, going to bed without being scared, etc.) remove a piece of "hair" until sphere is "bald".
- **Additional Ideas**: see also Hairy Helper
- **Hint**: instead pipe cleaners, use yarn or licorice
- **Educational Benefit**: 3-dimensional shapes, measurement, biology
- **Optional Incentive**: grow a Chia-Pet

Bountiful Blessings

"Give thanks to the Lord, for He is good;
His love endures forever."
Psalm 118:1

- **Goal**: thankfulness
- **Preparation Time**: 5-10 minutes
- **Materials Needed**: copy of following page, pictures of food cut out from grocery ads, glue, writing utensil
- **How to Use**: Write blessings or reasons to be thankful on food cut-outs and glue to cornucopia. At the end of each week, spend some time reading each item and thanking the Lord for His many blessings.
- **Additional Ideas**: record blessings all year and read at Thanksgiving
- **Hint**: laminate food cut-outs in order to wash off and reuse, or use large food stickers
- **Educational Benefit**: recognizing and naming various foods, writing
- **Optional Incentive**: go to family farm and pick some seasonal fruit or vegetables

Butterfly Kisses

"…I have loved you with an everlasting love;
I have drawn you with unfailing kindness."
Jeremiah 31:3

- **Goal**: kindness / love
- **Preparation Time**: 0-5 minutes
- **Materials Needed**: copy of following page, bits of colored tissue paper and glue, or crayons
- **How to Use**: Explain how butterflies change from plain caterpillars into beautiful butterflies, and how our hearts will change and become more beautiful each time we show love and kindness. Glue small pieces of tissue paper onto the butterfly each time child shows love (or have child color in sections of the butterfly).
- **Additional Ideas**: have child put on colored lip gloss and "kiss" butterfly each time love is shown, or have butterfly container filled with chocolate kisses that child may eat
- **Hint**: take it further by writing the love/kindness shown on each section of the butterfly
- **Educational Benefit**: art, science
- **Optional Incentive**: visit a terrarium (butterfly exhibit), eat some chocolate kisses (see Additional Ideas)

Building Blocks

"Knowledge puffs up, while love builds up."
1 Corinthians 8:1b

- **Goal**: encouragement
- **Preparation Time**: 0-5 minutes
- **Materials Needed**: alphabet blocks (letters Ex2,N,C,O,U,R,A,G)
- **How to Use**: Each time child builds someone up/encourages another, stack a block one letter at a time until the word "encourage" is spelled out (remove a block when child tears someone down/discourages another).
- **Additional Ideas**: spell child's name or the word "love" instead of "encourage"
- **Hint**: use glue dots to keep blocks from falling
- **Educational Benefit**: spatial reasoning, hand/eye coordination
- **Optional Incentive**: play Jenga

Button Basket

"…I will help you speak and will teach you what to say."
Exodus 4:12

- **Goal**: tone of voice / self-control
- **Preparation Time**: 0-5 minutes
- **Materials Needed**: 2 small baskets or jars, buttons (10/child + 10 extra), writing utensil
- **How to Use**: Have child(ren) count out 10 buttons to put in a small basket and label with name. Place the extra 10 buttons in 2nd basket. Each time kind words are used (or other self-control actions), take a button from the 2nd basket and give to child to put in his/her basket. When child chooses to be bossy, he/she must put one of their buttons back into the 2nd basket (optional). After predetermined amount of time (such as 1 week), count the buttons. Goal is to have at least 10 (or other such predetermined number).
- **Additional Ideas**: use buttons with 2 holes and draw a smiley face to remind child to use a happy tone of voice
- **Hint**: use for any other specific or general behavior (see Behavior Beans)
- **Educational Benefit**: counting, addition/subtraction
- **Optional Incentive**: exchange buttons for quarters and donate to favorite charity

Call Me

"The Lord is near to all who call on Him,
to all who call on Him in truth."
Psalm 145:18

- **Goal**: prayer
- **Preparation Time**: 0-5 minutes
- **Materials Needed**: copy of following page, crayon or marker
- **How to Use**: Encourage child to initiate "calling" God (i.e. pray) for anything…meals, bedtime, frustrations, praises, etc. Each time prayer is initiated by child, have child color in a cross on the cell phone.
- **Additional Ideas**: put stickers on an old cell or toy phone
- **Hint**: cut a phone shape out of a finished cereal box and draw buttons for each initiated prayer
- **Educational Benefit**: communication, counting
- **Optional Incentive**: allow child to call someone special and share Psalm 145:18 and what they've learned from the verse

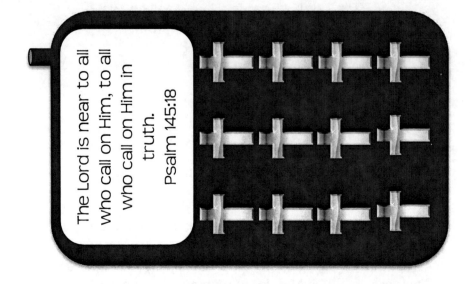

Caring Caterpillar

"Children…should learn first of all to put their religion into practice by caring for their own family…
for this is pleasing to God."
1 Timothy 5:4

- **Goal**: kindness / caring
- **Preparation Time**: 10-20 minutes
- **Materials Needed**: sticky back foam cut into circles, permanent marker, empty wall
- **How to Use**: Create a foam caterpillar face and attach toward the end of an empty wall. Each time child demonstrates caring for someone else, write it on the foam circle and attach to caterpillar's ever-growing body on the wall.
- **Additional Ideas**: see also Love Reporter for winter, and create a Peaceful Pumpkin Patch for autumn and a Beehaving Hive for summer
- **Hint**: for individual child, use round stickers to create the caterpillar on a sheet of paper and write the date of care demonstrated on given sticker
- **Educational Benefit**: study the life cycle of caterpillars/butterflies
- **Optional Incentive**: visit a butterfly farm (terrarium)

Caring Clover

But God has so composed the body…that there may be no division in the body, but that the members may have the same care for one another."
1 Corinthians 12:24b-25 (ESV)

- **Goal**: kindness / caring
- **Preparation Time**: 5-10 minutes
- **Materials Needed**: paper or cardboard, scissors, marker, ruler (optional)
- **How to Use**: Cut out a large clover from cardboard, then divide into 8 equal sections with a marker. Each time child demonstrates an example of caring, write it down in one section of the clover and color in until all 8 sections are filled.
- **Additional Ideas**: Before beginning, write an example of caring in each section and color in when child demonstrates.
- **Hint**: use the same way, but cut and divide a cross instead of the clover for "caring cross"
- **Educational Benefit**: fractions (dividing into equal parts)
- **Optional Incentive**: pick some flowers and give to elderly at retirement home (or think of another act of caring)

Catch Praise

"Be devoted to one another in love.
Honor one another above yourselves."
Romans 12:10

- **Goal**: encouragement
- **Preparation Time**: 5-10 minutes
- **Materials Needed**: index cards, hole punch, writing utensils, binder rings
- **How to Use**: Punch holes in the corner of each index card. Give each child an index card on which to decorate and write name, then attach to a binder ring. Encourage children to be devoted to each other by "catching" siblings doing something honorable or praiseworthy. They then write it on an index card and add it to sibling's binder ring.
- **Additional Ideas**: Pre-write praises or honorable deeds on cards, then when children catch each other being good, they give them the appropriate card to add to binder ring.
- **Hint**: For younger children, write out appropriate honorable deeds on cards for each child, then encourage siblings to "catch" them doing one and put a sticker on that child's card.
- **Educational Benefit**: writing, reading, fine motor skills
- **Optional Incentive**: play Catch Phrase by Milton Bradley

Caterpillar Countdown

"…Do not imitate what is evil but what is good. Anyone who does what is good is from God."
3 John 1:11

- **Goal**: behavior
- **Preparation Time**: 5-10 minutes
- **Materials Needed**: construction paper, scissors, writing utensil (or letter stickers), tape, circle shape to trace
- **How to Use**: Determine behavior goals, cut out one circle per goal, then write goal on each circle. Tape together to create caterpillar (leave one circle for face and let child decorate). As child achieves goal(s), remove one circle at a time until only head remains.
- **Additional Ideas**: set one behavior goal and cut out a circle for each letter of that goal
- **Hint**: Use plain round stickers and write one goal per sticker or one letter of goal per sticker. As child achieves goal, attach appropriate circle to create caterpillar's body.
- **Educational Benefit**: counting, spelling
- **Optional Incentive**: make a caterpillar using round cookies and writable frosting, or round crackers and squeeze cheese

Chocolate Lovers

"I have hidden Your Word in my heart
that I might not sin against You."
Psalm 119:11

- **Goal**: love
- **Preparation Time**: 10-20 minutes
- **Materials Needed**: copy of following page, scissors, cardboard
- **How to Use**: Cut out Chocolate Lovers candy kisses and a large heart out of cardboard. Glue a candy kiss onto the heart each time child shows love (or cover the heart with real Hershey's Kisses and child may eat one each time love is shown).
- **Additional Ideas**: Write memory verses on one side of candy kiss cut-outs and references on the other, then put in a bag. Pull one candy kiss out of the bag and work on memorizing. When all (or each) are memorized, earn a real Hershey's Kiss.
- **Hint**: use a heart-shaped box of chocolates (buy on sale after Valentine's Day)
- **Educational Benefit**: reading, memorization, addition/subtraction
- **Optional Incentive**: see Hint

Chocolate Lovers

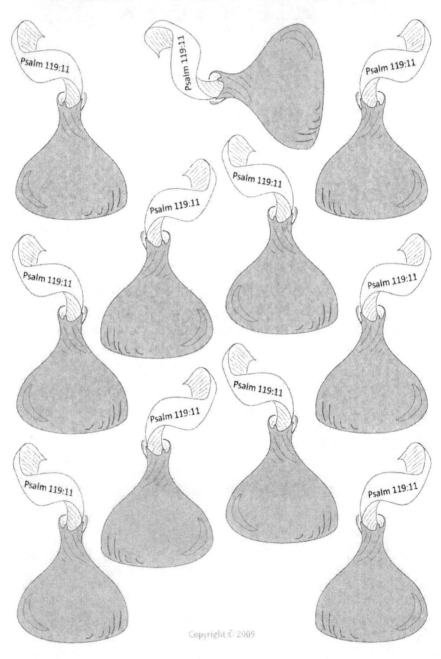

Chore Champ

"I press on toward the goal to win the prize for which God has called me heavenward in Christ Jesus."
Philippians 3:14

- **Goal**: responsibility
- **Preparation Time**: 5-10 minutes
- **Materials Needed**: cardboard, foil, yellow paper (or copy of following page), marker, scissors, tape, 5 safety pins
- **How to Use**: Cut out 5 circles from yellow paper and write a chore on each one. Cut out 5 triangles from cardboard and wrap in foil. In large capital letters, write one letter of the word CHAMP on each piece of foil. Connect triangles and circles to look like medals. Each time child shows responsibility by completing a chore before being reminded, allow child to be a Chore Champ for the rest of the day by wearing the appropriate medal.
- **Additional Ideas**: cut out a picture of child and make gold medal ribbons to put around neck, or make a list of chores then glue small pictures of child(ren) onto medals and put next to each chore they complete
- **Hint**: purchase trophy stickers or blue ribbons
- **Educational Benefit**: spelling, reading, sight words
- **Optional Incentive**: take child to watch a sports game (or participate in one)

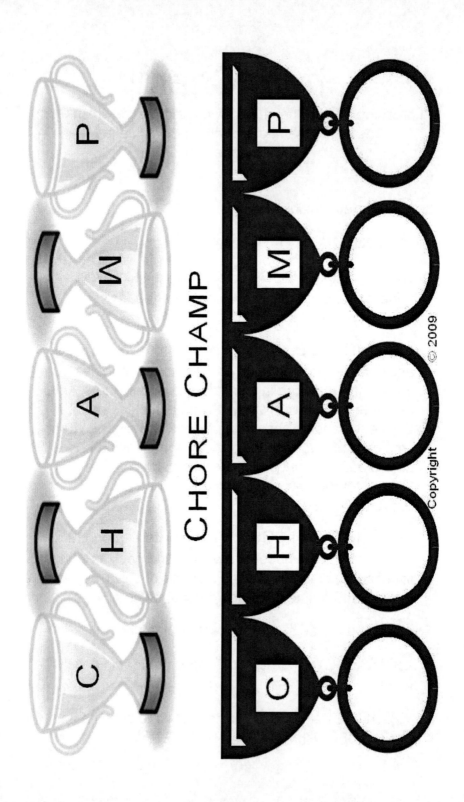

Cheery O's

"A happy heart makes the face cheerful."
Proverbs 15:13

- **Goal**: joyfulness
- **Preparation Time**: 0-5 minutes
- **Materials Needed**: Cheerios, small jar or yarn
- **How to Use**: Fill a jar or string a necklace with Cheerios. Child may eat one Cheerio each time cheerfulness is demonstrated until the Cheerios are all eaten. That's a lot of cheerfulness!
- **Additional Ideas**: add to jar or necklace with cheerios each time child gives /shares cheerfully (or use when obeying cheerfully)
- **Hint**: if necklace, hang somewhere safe instead of wearing
- **Educational Benefit**: counting, addition, subtraction
- **Optional Incentive**: fry some cheerios in a pan with a butter and parmesan cheese to enjoy a delicious snack (my mom's favorite)

Clean Heart

"Cleanse me…and I will be clean;
wash me, and I will be whiter than snow."
Psalm 51:7b

- **Goal**: attitude
- **Preparation Time**: 5-10 minutes
- **Materials Needed**: plastic grocery bag (mostly white), black vis-à-vis, tongs, large jar, water
- **How to Use**: Cut out several hearts from the grocery bag. Color each heart with a black vis-à-vis. As child shows a changed/clean heart, dip the black heart into a jar of water with tongs and watch how it turns from black to white (just like Jesus washes our hearts white as snow).
- **Additional Ideas**: instead of coloring entire heart, write various behaviors needing improvement on hearts and "wash clean" when improvement is shown
- **Hint**: look for sturdier plastic hearts at a craft store
- **Educational Benefit**: reading, writing, scientific diffusion
- **Optional Incentive**: enjoy some candy hearts

Color by Number

"Teach us to number our days,
that we may gain a heart of wisdom."
Psalm 90:12

- **Goal**: wise choices
- **Preparation Time**: 0-5 minutes
- **Materials Needed**: color by number page (found in craft stores in children section), coloring utensils
- **How to Use**: Child may color all the sections of one number on the picture each time child demonstrates a heart of wisdom (making good choices, using self-control, obeying, etc.).
- **Additional Ideas**: see also Heart of Wisdom
- **Hint**: use a page from a coloring book and have child color one section at a time
- **Educational Benefit**: number and color recognition, fine motor skills
- **Optional Incentive**: play hopscotch and stop to say a word from Psalm 90:12 in each square

Complaint Can

"Those who are wayward in spirit will gain understanding;
those who complain will accept instruction."
Isaiah 29:24

- **Goal**: peace
- **Preparation Time**: 0-5 minutes
- **Materials Needed**: empty Crystal Light container (label "Complaint Can"), scrap paper, writing utensil (readily available)
- **How to Use**: Instead of child verbally complaining, direct child to write frustration/complaint on a piece of scrap paper and put in the Complaint Can. Check box each night together and decide on a solution.
- **Additional Ideas**: if children are too young to write, encourage them to illustrate their complaint or ask older sibling to write it for them (see also Frustration Station)
- **Hint**: *Please remember*—if it's important enough for child to write down, then take it seriously, no matter how insignificant it might seem
- **Educational Benefit**: writing/drawing, problem-solving
- **Optional Incentive**: allow child to help take out the trash or sort the recycling—believe it or not, this can be quite fun!

Cookie Jar

"The world and its desires pass away, but whoever does the will of God lives forever."
1 John 2:17

- **Goal:** behavior
- **Preparation Time:** 0-5 minutes
- **Materials Needed:** copy of following page, Cookie Crisp cereal, tube frosting (as glue), writing utensil
- **How to Use:** Decide on a behavior goal and write it on the lid of cookie jar. "Glue" on a predetermined number of cookie cereal pieces. As child demonstrates the desired behavior, remove a cookie from the jar and eat, if desired. Continue until all of the cookies have been eaten/removed.
- **Additional Ideas:** Cut out brown circles as cookies and write various goals on each cookie. As child demonstrates, glue on jar until full.
- **Hint:** for younger (or pickier) children, draw circles onto Cookie Jar then have child color in circles each time instead of eating cereal
- **Educational Benefit:** sorting, counting, estimating
- **Optional Incentive:** bake some cookies together and enjoy dipping them in milk

Cookie Jar

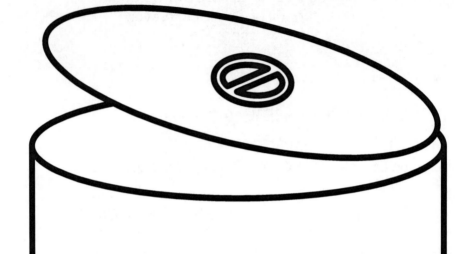

The world and its desires pass away,
but whoever does the will of God lives forever.
1 John 2:17

Cookie Press

"I press on to take hold of that for which
Christ Jesus took hold of me."
Philippians 3:12b

- **Goal**: behavior
- **Preparation Time**: 0-5 minutes (grocery run may be necessary)
- **Materials Needed**: ingredients to make child's favorite cookies (more for older children, fewer for younger children)
- **How to Use**: Choose a goal behavior for child. Each day child accomplishes goal, child chooses one ingredient to set aside for the cookies. When child has earned all the ingredients, make the cookies together.
- **Additional Ideas**: Print a large picture of a cookie and cut into pieces according to the number of ingredients needed. Write ingredient on back of each piece. Child puts cookie together until complete.
- **Hint**: for younger children have cookies premade, then child chooses topping to put on cookie (e.g. sprinkles, sugar, frosting, etc.)
- **Educational Benefit**: reading (ingredients), science, math (measurement)
- **Optional Incentive**: take some homemade cookies to a neighbor or teacher

Cross Stitch

"For the message of the cross is foolishness to those who are perishing, but to us who are being saved it is the power of God."
1 Corinthians 1:18

- **Goal**: behavior
- **Preparation Time**: 5-10 minutes
- **Materials Needed**: cardstock, hole punch, twist-ties or yarn cut into 1" lengths
- **How to Use**: Decide on goal (see Additional Ideas) and cut out appropriate number of squares. Punch 1-2 holes at the bottom of each square, depending on size. Each time goal is accomplished, "stitch" squares together with yarn or twist-ties to form a cross.
- **Additional Ideas**: use for behavior, responsibility, Scripture memory, etc. as individual goals or one goal spelling out each letter on a square
- **Hint**: use empty cereal box, felt scraps, or foam paper instead of cardstock
- **Educational Benefit**: spelling, eye-hand coordination
- **Optional Incentive**: allow child to really "stitch" something using a blunt needle or child's sewing kit (found in craft or toy stores)

Cooperation Coordinates

"Live in harmony with one another."
Romans 12:16

- **Goal**: cooperation
- **Preparation Time**: 15-20 minutes
- **Materials Needed**: copy of following grid, tape, photo/picture/clip-art (approx. 4x6 ¾"), scissors, writing utensil
- **How to Use**: Cut picture into 25 squares to match grid dimensions. Label the back of each square with its correct coordinate (e.g. "B3"—down, then across). As child shows cooperation, give a square to attach to the grid. Success is achieved when all squares have been posted and picture is complete.
- **Additional Ideas**: Have a monthly themed picture and set goal to complete picture in a month. For multiple children use a photo of each child and have children "race" to see who will complete their grid first.
- **Hint**: in order to reuse, laminate grid and picture(s), then use sticky tac to attach
- **Educational Benefit**: coordinates, graphing, plotting
- **Optional Incentive**: go on a walk and create a neighborhood map using coordinates

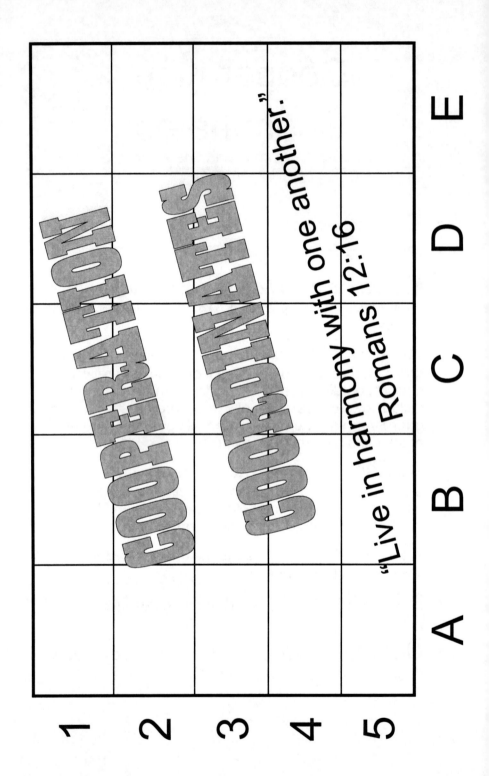

Crown Him with Many Crayons

"Who is he, this King of glory?
The Lord Almighty—He is the King of glory."
Psalm 24:10

- **Goal**: attitude
- **Preparation Time**: 0-5 minutes
- **Materials Needed**: empty cereal box cut in ½ lengthwise (to fit around child's head as crown), hot glue gun and glue, crayons
- **How to Use**: As child demonstrates a Christ-like (Kingly) attitude, hot glue a crayon to child's crown. When crown is covered with pre-determined number of crayon jewels, child may be "crowned a king".
  Note: Size the crown to fit child's head, but don't allow child to wear until goal is met.
- **Additional Ideas**: make jewels out of old crayons by removing the wrappers, melting in microwave in mini baking cups, and letting cool completely before gluing onto crown
- **Hint**: many craft stores carry plain crowns to decorate, or ask for one at Burger King
- **Educational Benefit**: counting, measuring, science
- **Optional Incentive**: eat at Burger King or Dairy Queen, have a Knight Dubbing Ceremony or Royal Tea Party

Delight Brite

"The Lord detests lying lips, but He delights in people who are trustworthy."
Proverbs 12:22

- **Goal**: honesty
- **Preparation Time**: 0-5 minutes
- **Materials Needed**: Lite Brite and pegs (by Hasbro)
- **How to Use**: Add a peg to the Lite Brite each time honesty is demonstrated, eventually spelling out the word "truth".
- **Additional Ideas**: use to spell out any other specific behavior, or spell out child's name when general positive behavior is demonstrated.
- **Hint**: if one peg at a time is taking too long, have child spell out one letter at time (or purchase L.B. letters online from the Hasbro website)
- **Educational Benefit**: spelling
- **Optional Incentive**: Lite Brite free play!

Doer Daisy

"Do not merely listen to the word and so deceive yourselves. Do what it says."
James 1:22

- **Goal**: self-initiative / thoughtfulness
- **Preparation Time**: 0-5 minutes
- **Materials Needed**: copy of following page (one complete flower and flower head per child), scissors, coloring utensils
- **How to Use**: Color stem and pot on Doer Daisy and write child's name on the pot. Color and cut apart the petals from flower head. Each time child is a *doer* and not just a *hearer* of God's Word, write it down on a loose petal then glue that petal onto the Doer Daisy. When flower is complete reflect on each way child was a doer of God's Word.
- **Additional Ideas**: glue actual flower petals onto the Doer Daisy
- **Hint**: child may color in each petal instead of gluing each one onto the flower
- **Educational Benefit**: ordering, completing puzzle
- **Optional Incentive**: pick or plant flowers together

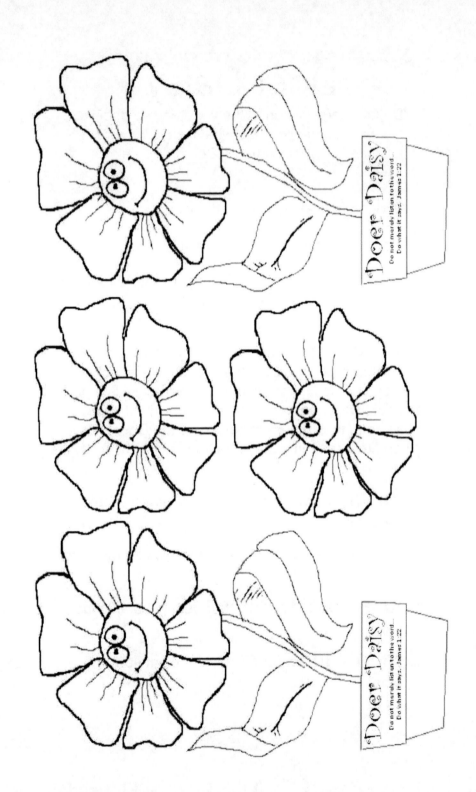

Do-Unto's

"Do [un]to others as you would have them do [un]to you."
Luke 6:31

- **Goal**: self-control / peace
- **Preparation Time**: 5-10 minutes
- **Materials Needed**: brown paper or thin cardboard, scissors, plate, crayon shavings or glitter (for sprinkles), glue
- **How to Use**: Cut out 12 circles with a smaller circle cut out of the center (like a donut). Each time child demonstrates self-control by thinking *before* reacting, write it on the "donut" (a.k.a. do-unto), then have child glue on "sprinkles" (crayon shavings or glitter) and put it on the plate. Goal is to fill up the plate with one dozen do-unto's.
- **Additional Ideas**: remove do-unto's each time child loses self-control
- **Hint**: if using crayon shavings, place sprinkled do-unto between two pieces of wax paper and iron on low
- **Educational Benefit**: art, shapes
- **Optional Incentive**: have real donuts for breakfast or dessert when child fills up do-unto's plate

Dream Weaver

"A dream comes when there are many cares, and many words mark the speech of a fool."
Ecclesiastes 5:3

- **Goal**: peace
- **Preparation Time**: 10-15 minutes
- **Materials Needed**: 2-3 sheets of colored of construction paper, one black sheet (for mat), scissors, glue
- **How to Use**: Fold one sheet of paper in ½ lengthwise. Cut slits 1" apart, leaving a ½" border around each side. Cut the other colored sheets into 1" strips lengthwise. When child demonstrates peace (not arguing, sharing toy, calming frustrated sibling, etc.), give one strip to weave through the mat, sliding it all the way up each time and gluing on either end. Goal is to complete the mat.
- **Additional Ideas**: make thicker strips for younger children and thinner strips for older children and vary the shape of the weave mat
- **Hint**: buy weaving crafts at orientaltrading.com
- **Educational Benefit**: fine motor skills
- **Optional Incentive**: laminate and use as placemat for meal time

Dress-a-Bear

"Therefore, as God's chosen people, holy and dearly loved, clothe yourselves with compassion, kindness, humility, gentleness and patience."
Colossians 3:12

- **Goal**: Scripture application
- **Preparation Time**: 5-10 minutes
- **Materials Needed**: following page traced onto foam or felt, scissors, coloring utensils, Velcro (if using foam), or see Hint
- **How to Use**: Have child color and cut out bear and clothing. Each time child demonstrates a characteristic from Colossians 3:12, give appropriate piece of clothing for child to dress the bear. Goal is achieved when bear is completely clothed.
- **Additional Ideas**: dress a pumpkin with Mr. Potato Head pieces for fall, a butterfly for spring, and an octopus for summer
- **Hint**: copy bear and clothing onto construction paper and use glue sticks
- **Educational Benefit**: vocabulary, getting dressed
- **Optional Incentive**: visit a build-a-bear workshop

Encouragement Elephant

"Encourage one another and build each other up."
1 Thessalonians 5:11a

- **Goal**: encouragement
- **Preparation Time**: 5-10 minutes
- **Materials Needed**: copy of following page (have child color), photo of child that fits elephant's sign
- **How to Use**: Cut the photo into puzzle pieces (see Hint). Each time child encourages someone, glue a piece of the photo onto the elephant's sign until the photo puzzle is complete.
- **Additional Ideas**: Use a stuffed elephant that child may take to nap, bed, dinner, errand, etc. when child has been encouraging.
- **Hint**: Determine ahead of time how many pieces to cut from photo (for younger children, cut simple lines and few pieces, for older children, be creative or let them cut apart their own).
- **Educational Benefit**: logic, matching parts, completing puzzle
- **Optional Incentive**: go to the zoo and see the elephants, or put a large puzzle together as a family

Encouragement Elephant
"Encourage one another and build each other up."
1 Thessalonians 5:11a

Eggs-actly!

"Children, obey your parents in everything,
for this pleases the Lord."
Colossians 3:20

- **Goal**: obedience
- **Preparation Time**: 5-10 minutes
- **Materials Needed**: plastic eggs, small strips of paper, writing utensil, basket or empty egg carton, prizes (optional)
- **How to Use**: Each time child obeys *exactly* as directed, write it down on strips of paper, place it in an egg, and put it in the basket/carton. Goal is achieved when the basket/carton is filled with predetermined number of eggs.
- **Additional Ideas**: Place predetermined "prizes" in each egg. When child obeys exactly as directed, child opens an egg and receives a treat (find inexpensive plastic eggs after Easter).
- **Hint**: cut out ovals as eggs, recycle a paper grocery bag to make a nest, then write on backside of the eggs and let child decorate and glue onto nest
- **Educational Benefit**: writing/reading, shapes (oval, ovoid), counting
- **Optional Incentive**: make omelets for breakfast or decorate some hard-boiled eggs

Fearless Freddy

"For the Spirit God gave us does not make us timid, but gives us power, love and self-discipline."
2 Timothy 1:7

- **Goal**: Scripture application / confidence
- **Preparation Time**: 0-5 minutes
- **Materials Needed**: Mr. Potato Head & pieces
- **How to Use**: Each time child demonstrates a spirit of self-confidence, love, or self-discipline give a piece to "dress" Mr. Potato Head (a.k.a. Freddy)
- **Additional Ideas**: see also Behavior Baldy or Hairy Helper
- **Hint**: create "Freddy" out of construction paper, and draw clothing each time a characteristic above is demonstrated (see also Dress-a-Bear)
- **Educational Benefit**: do a science experiment with a real potato
- **Optional Incentive**: make some homemade fries or potato chips

Faithful "Fall"ower

"Let love and faithfulness never leave you."
Proverbs 3:3a

- **Goal**: wise choices (following Jesus)
- **Preparation Time**: 5-10 minutes
- **Materials Needed**: color a copy of following page (or create larger tree on cardboard and use 12 leaf stickers or go on "leaf hunt" to collect some in various fall colors), paperclips, scissors
- **How to Use**: Place the Faithful Tree somewhere visible. Each time child shows faithfulness (e.g. praying for a friend, giving away a toy, etc.) write it on leaf and paperclip to the tree.
- **Additional Ideas**: write examples of faithfulness on each tree limb, then attach leaf when child demonstrates that example
- **Hint**: use for Scripture memory by writing reference on tree leaves and gluing on leaf when child memorizes that particular verse
- **Educational Benefit**: seasons (autumn), colors
- **Optional Incentive**: enjoy the fall season by raking the leaves for an elderly person or going on a nature walk to see all the shapes, sizes and colors of leaves

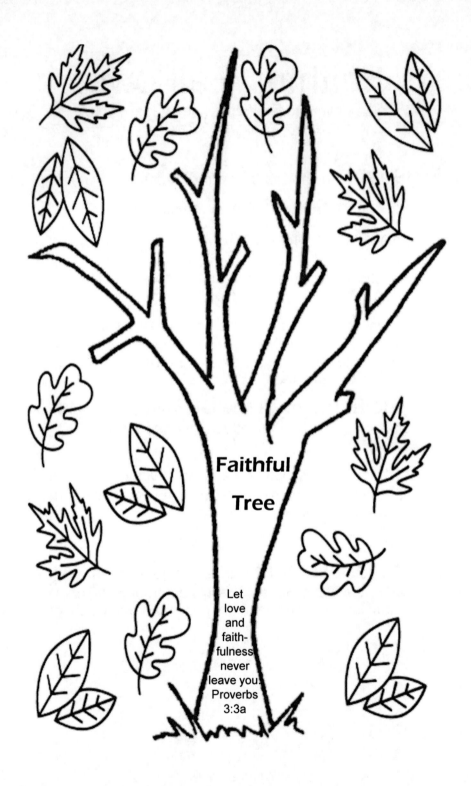

Fisher of Men

"'Come, follow me,' Jesus said, 'and I will send you out to fish for people.'
At once they left their nets and followed him."
Matthew 4:19-20

- **Goal**: wise choices (following Jesus)
- **Preparation Time**: 0-5 minutes
- **Materials Needed**: copy of following page, 7-10 pieces of string cut into 3" lengths and tape, or fish stickers (see Hint)
- **How to Use**: Attach a piece of string from the fishing pole toward the fish each time child makes a wise choice which demonstrates following Jesus.
- **Additional Ideas**: draw large fish on poster board, write wise choices that child made on post-its and stick on fish as "scales" until fish is covered
- **Hint**: use fish stickers to place on fish instead of string from the fishing pole
- **Educational Benefit**: counting
- **Optional Incentive**: eat goldfish crackers for snack, play "Go Fish", purchase live fish as a visual reminder to be a Fisher of Men

Fisher of Men

"Come, follow me," Jesus said, "and I will send you out to fish for people." At once they left their nets and followed him.

Matthew 4:19-20

Fix-It Shop

"For if you forgive other people when they sin against you, your heavenly Father will also forgive you."
Matthew 6:14

- **Goal**: forgiveness
- **Preparation Time**: 0-5 minutes
- **Materials Needed**: copy of following page with each tool cut apart (or see Hint), 8 small nails, wood (L=1.5"), hammer
  Keep real tools out of reach of child and only do this with adult supervision!
- **How to Use**: As child demonstrates forgiveness toward others, asking for forgiveness, or independently correcting a wrong choice, nail a tool onto the wood (in correct order) to spell out "FORGIVER".
- **Additional Ideas**: discuss how each tool has a special use just like we are each special to God
- **Hint**: use plastic tools found at dollar store and write a letter on each one as child demonstrates forgiveness
- **Educational Benefit**: tool uses and letter recognition
- **Optional Incentive**: build a bird house together

FIX-IT SHOP

For if you forgive other people when they sin against you, your heavenly Father will also forgive you.
Matthew 6:14

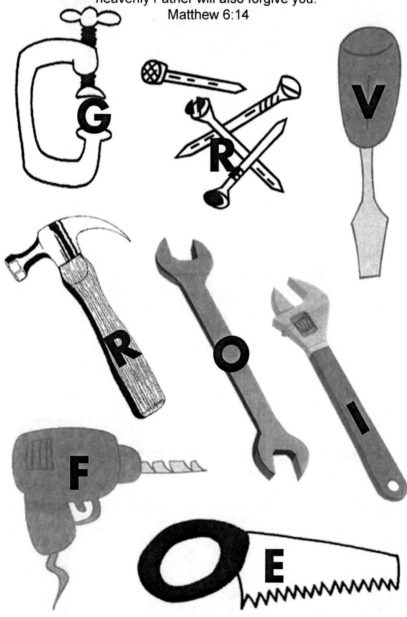

Fill 'er Up

"May the God of hope fill you with all <u>joy</u> and <u>peace</u> as you <u>trust</u> in Him, so that you may overflow with <u>hope</u> by the power of the Holy Spirit."
Romans 15:13

- **Goal**: Scripture application
- **Preparation Time**: 0-5 minutes
- **Materials Needed**: picture of fuel tank with at least 3 marks between Empty and Full, paperclip
- **How to Use**: Place paperclip on fuel tank at Empty. Remind children that just as it takes fuel (gasoline) to keep a car going, it takes fuel (trust, hope, peace, joy in God) to keep a person going and that without God we are empty. Each time child demonstrates one of the underlined words in the verse, move one section closer to Full. Goal is to go from Empty to Full (and on to overflowing).
- **Additional Ideas**: for younger children, give specific examples of joy, peace, trust and hope to achieve
- **Hint**: if child demonstrates opposite behavior, move the gas tank lever toward Empty
- **Educational Benefit**: understanding opposites
- **Optional Incentive**: next time your fuel tank is low, have child help add fuel (point out to them how the tank moves toward full)

Flower Power

"Devote yourselves to prayer,
being watchful and thankful."
Colossians 4:2

- **Goal**: prayer
- **Preparation Time**: 5-10 minutes
- **Materials Needed**: small flower pot, craft sticks, tape, writing utensil, scissors, foam cut to fit in flower pot (optional)
- **How to Use**: Tape a friend's picture on top of each craft stick, and place in the flower pot. Focus on one name each day for whom child should pray.
- **Additional Ideas**: write requests on the front and answered prayers on the back or date of started/answered prayer request
- **Hint**: encourage child to paint and decorate flower pot
- **Educational Benefit**: sight words, spelling
- **Optional Incentive**: plant or pick a flower for each friend

Friendship Fish

"A friend loves at all times."
Proverbs 17:17a

- **Goal**: kindness
- **Preparation Time**: 0-5 minutes
- **Materials Needed**: copy of following page, photos of friend
- **How to Use**: Have child decorate Friendship Fish and copy onto cardstock (laminate if available). Each week post a picture of a friend on the fish's body. Be a loving friend by praying for, writing a letter or sending an email to, visiting, giving a gift to, etc. your friend of the week.
- **Additional Ideas**: Use your church, school, or neighborhood directory to familiarize yourselves with other members in your community and/or use for missionaries or church leaders.
- **Hint**: save pictures from Christmas letters to use throughout the year
- **Educational Benefit**: writing, conversation
- **Optional Incentive**: call the friend for whom you've been praying

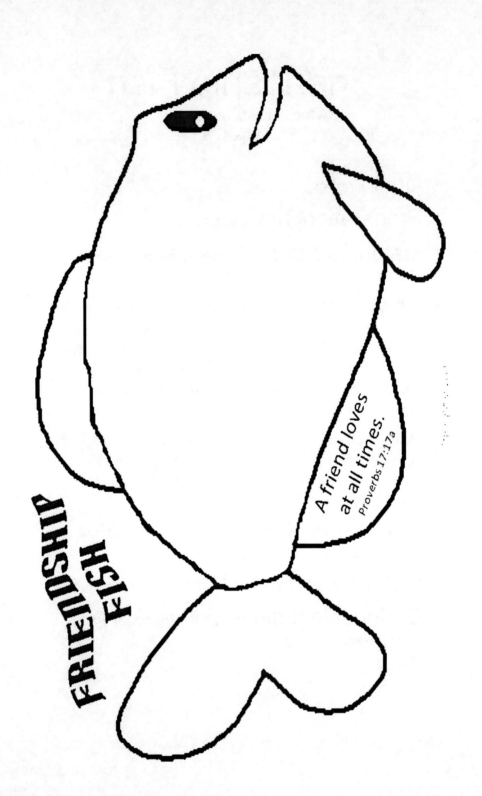

Fruit of the Spirit Tree

"The fruit of the Spirit is love, joy, peace, patience, kindness, goodness, faithfulness, gentleness and self-control."
Galatians 5:22-23

- **Goal**: Scripture application
- **Preparation Time**: 0-5 minutes
- **Materials Needed**: copy of following page, fruit stickers, coloring utensils to color tree
- **How to Use**: As child demonstrates a "fruit" of the Spirit (see Bible verse), put a sticker on the appropriate section of the tree until each section has at least one sticker.
- **Additional Ideas**: For multiple siblings, use tree when showing teamwork in each area, then add flowers underneath the tree for individual behaviors.
- **Hint**: fill one fruit at a time until tree is complete or place multiple fruit stickers on one behavior each time demonstrated and discuss which fruits were easier to accomplish and which were more difficult
- **Educational Benefit**: sight words, reading, counting, comparing
- **Optional Incentive**: make a fruit salad together to enjoy as snack or go to a farm and pick some fruit

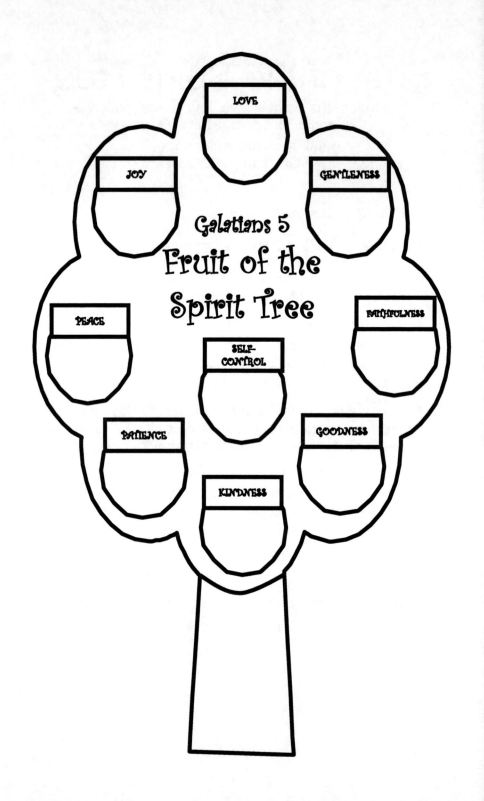

Friends Fries

"…he pleads with God as one pleads for a friend."
Job 16:21

- **Goal**: prayer
- **Preparation Time**: 5-10 minutes
- **Materials Needed**: unused french fry container, large craft sticks, permanent marker
- **How to Use**: Write the name of a friend on each craft stick and place in the fry container. Pull out one craft stick per day and have child pray for that friend.
- **Additional Ideas**: write requests on the front and answered prayers on the back or date of started/answered prayer request
- **Hint**: ask for a french fry container at a fast food restaurant
- **Educational Benefit**: sight words and spelling
- **Optional Incentive**: take a friend out for some fries and tell him/her about Jesus and/or share answered prayers

Frustration Station

"For everything that was written in the past was written to teach us, so that through the endurance taught in the Scriptures and the encouragement they provide we might have hope."
Romans 15:4

- **Goal**: peace (reduce tattling)
- **Preparation Time**: 0-5 minutes
- **Materials Needed**: notebook, or empty container and slips of paper, writing utensil
- **How to Use**: Set aside a special area called the "Frustration Station". When child is frustrated about something or someone, he/she should write it down in either the notebook or on slips of paper to put in container at the "Frustration Station". At a set time *daily*, review the frustrations, discuss possible solutions, and pray with person(s) involved.
- **Additional Ideas**: Encourage older children to write using complete sentences. Encourage younger children to draw a picture of the frustrating situation.
- **Hint**: Remind children that this replaces verbal tattling and is only to be used when situation is truly frustrating and can't seem to be resolved quickly.
- **Educational Benefit**: writing, journaling, drawing
- **Optional Incentive**: If frustrations are resolved independently (or you notice a significant reduction in tattling), replace the "Frustration Station" with cookies and label "Celebration Station".

Get Up!
"…Rise up and stand firm!"
Psalm 20:8b

- **Goal**: self-initiative
- **Preparation Time**: 10-15 minutes
- **Materials Needed**: pillowcase, copy of following page on iron-on transfer sheet (or see hint)
- **How to Use**: Cut the following page down the middle and iron one on both sides of the pillowcase. Each time self-initiative is demonstrated, child should flip pillowcase to the awake side. Each time laziness is demonstrated, flip pillowcase to sleeping side. Goal is to end the day with pillowcase on awake (non-lazy) side.
- **Additional Ideas**: use for attitude or any other behavior with a happy/smiling face on one side and a sad/frowning face on the other
- **Hint**: have child appropriately design/decorate each side of the pillow with permanent or fabric markers
- **Educational Benefit**: opposites, art
- **Optional Incentive**: when pillowcase stays on non-lazy side, allow child to stay up a bit past bedtime

GET UP!

...The lazy person turns over in bed.
Proverbs 26:14 (NLT)

GET UP!

...Rise up and stand firm!
Psalm 20:8b

Glad-Libs

"My heart is glad and my tongue rejoices."
Psalm 16:9

- **Goal**: joyfulness
- **Preparation Time**: 10-20 minutes
- **Materials Needed**: paper and writing utensil (or computer)
- **How to Use**: Create a "Glad-Lib" by making up a story about child and leaving blanks for certain parts of speech. Each time child demonstrates thankfulness, gladness, praise, etc., let child choose a word to fill in until Glad-Lib is complete (see example).

  "Once upon a time there was a _____ (noun) named _____ (person's name). On _____ (day), _____ (name) gave thanks to God for _____ (verb). On _____ (another day), _____ (name) gave thanks to God for his _____ (adjective) _____ (noun). On _____ (day), _____ (name) gave thanks to God for _____ (verb ending in "ing"), and so on…

- **Additional Ideas**: Put words in a bag and have child pull one out and fill in appropriate place in Glad-Lib.
- **Hint**: type and save on computer to reuse again
- **Educational Benefit**: parts of speech, spelling, creative writing, reading comprehension
- **Optional Incentive**: write some Glad-Libs as a family for another time

God Rocks!

"I tell you," He replied, "if they [the disciples] keep quiet, the stones will cry out."
Luke 19:40

- **Goal**: thankfulness
- **Preparation Time**: 0-5 minutes
- **Materials Needed**: small stones (pebbles), thin permanent marker, clear jar, bag
- **How to Use**: Keep clean, smooth stones in a bag near the jar. Each time child initiates thankfulness or praise to God, write it on a stone and place in the jar. Goal is to become comfortable praising God aloud.
- **Additional Ideas**: When children are having difficulty finding the positive in things purchase a large beach ball and pretend that it's a stone. Write a praises to God on each section. Have children toss the ball to each other and "cry out" the praise that their right hand lands on. After each praise, take a step backward. See how many praises they can cry out before they drop the "stone".
- **Hint**: use individual jars for multiple children and/or have older children write praises on the stones themselves
- **Educational Benefit**: spelling, gross motor skills (see Additional Ideas)
- **Optional Incentive**: play "I Spy God" wherever you are by "spying" things that God has done (e.g. I spy God because he prevented that car from bumping into us, I spy God in the beautiful colors of that rainbow…)

God's Team

"A hot-tempered person stirs up conflict,
but the one who is patient calms a quarrel."
Proverbs 15:18

- **Goal**: behavior
- **Preparation Time**: 0-5 minutes
- **Materials Needed**: copy of following page, small football shape, sticky tac, Teddy Grahams (optional), writing utensil
- **How to Use**: Write behaviors on goal lines, child's name on football (if more than one child) and place it on the 0-yard line (Old Behavior zone). Move football up toward goal behavior or down toward old behavior. Goal is to score a touchdown for God's Team by getting to the 100-yard line (Goal Behavior zone).
- **Additional Ideas**: Place Teddy Grahams (football players) at every 15 yards. When a player is reached (only when heading toward touchdown), child may eat it.
- **Hint**: change goal behavior based on current need
- **Educational Benefit**: counting by fives to 100
- **Optional Incentive**: play a family football game

God's Team Football Field

A hot-tempered person stirs up conflict, but the one who is patient calms a quarrel. Proverbs 15:18

	Goal Behavior	
100		100
95		95
90		90
85		85
80		80
75		75
70		70
65		65
60		60
55		55
50		50
45		45
40		40
35		35
30		30
25		25
20		20
15		15
10		10
5		5
0	Old Behavior	0

God's Handy-work

"The heavens declare the glory of God, and the sky above proclaims His handiwork."
Psalm 19:1 (ESV)

- **Goal**: behavior
- **Preparation Time**: 5-10 minutes
- **Materials Needed**: paper, writing utensil, washable stamp pad, scissors (optional)
- **How to Use**: Outline child's hand (cut out if desired). Write one goal on each finger. When child achieves that goal, use stamp pad to put child's fingerprint on that finger until the entire hand has fingerprints.
- **Additional Ideas**: use for prayer time or extra chores
- **Hint**: instead of stamping fingerprints use stickers as "fingernails" or "rings", or have child color each finger
- **Educational Benefit**: fingerprint science, art, fine motor skills
- **Optional Incentive**: Make edible finger paint with yogurt. Mix in different flavors of Kool-Aid for a variety of colors.

Grate-fullness

"Do everything without grumbling or arguing."
Philippians 2:14

- **Goal**: thankfulness / grateful attitude
- **Preparation Time**: 0-5 minutes
- **Materials Needed**: old crayons (wrappers removed), grater, small clear jar
- **How to Use**: Each time child shows humility and/or gratefulness, grate one crayon into jar. Goal is to fill up jar with crayon shavings.
- **Additional Ideas**: Grate crayons onto wax paper, cover with another piece of wax paper, iron on low, let cool, then cut out a design.
- **Hint**: purchase a grater from a dollar store
- **Educational Benefit**: art (see Additional Ideas)
- **Optional Incentive**: make a pizza together (be sure to grate the cheese)

GRRRattitude

"Let the message of Christ dwell among you richly as you teach and admonish one another with all wisdom through psalms, hymns, and songs from the Spirit, singing to God with gratitude in your hearts."
Colossians 3:16

- **Goal**: thankfulness / grateful attitude
- **Preparation Time**: 0-5 minutes
- **Materials Needed**: copy of following page (cut out one for each child to color), small round crackers (see Hint), frosting or peanut butter (as glue)
- **How to Use**: Each time child shows an attitude of gratitude, "glue" a cracker to the "mane" until full.
- **Additional Ideas**: Copy a picture of a tiger and color in stripes (or use black licorice) each time child shows gratefulness.
- **Hint**: Use larger crackers (e.g. Ritz) for short-term results or smaller crackers (e.g. Ritz Bits) to work on behavior longer.
- **Educational Benefit**: decorating, cutting, counting
- **Optional Incentive**: make an edible Grrrattitude Lion snack by cutting bread into a circle, cover with peanut butter, raisins and licorice to make its face, then surround with round crackers for mane

GRRRATTITUDE LION

Grow Up

"But grow in the grace and knowledge of
our Lord and Savior Jesus Christ."
2 Peter 3:18a

- **Goal**: behavior
- **Preparation Time**: 0-5 minutes
- **Materials Needed**: light blue paper, green pipe cleaners, tape (or glue gun), yellow marker or sticker of sun
- **How to Use**: Draw a yellow sun in the top corner of the paper and determine a behavior goal. Each time child demonstrates that behavior, tape a pipe cleaner growing from the bottom of the page up toward the sun (Son).
- **Additional Ideas**: use specifically for demonstrating grace or knowledge of the Lord
- **Hint**: draw green lines, or tape pipe cleaners all over page, then have child put flowers stickers on each one when goal is demonstrated
- **Educational Benefit**: read <u>Jack and the Beanstalk</u>
- **Optional Incentive**: plant some flowers or vegetables and watch them grow as they spend time in the sun

Hairy Helper

"…Whatever you do, do it all for the glory of God."
1 Corinthians 10:31b

- **Goal**: helpfulness
- **Preparation Time**: 5-10 minutes
- **Materials Needed**: small styrofoam sphere (found in craft sections) with face drawn on front, thick yarn or thin licorice (cut into ½" - 1" sections), toothpick
- **How to Use**: Each time child initiates helpfulness, add a piece of "hair" (yarn or licorice) to the sphere until the Hairy Helper is full.
- **Additional Ideas**: see also Boldness Baldy
- **Hint**: instead of yarn or licorice, use pipe cleaners cut into fourths to create spiky hair (keep out of reach of young children)
- **Educational Benefit**: 3-dimensional shapes, measurement, biology
- **Optional Incentive**: take care of a chia-pet

Hamburger Helper

"The Lord is with me; He is my helper."
Psalm 118:7a

- **Goal**: helpfulness
- **Preparation Time**: 10-15 minutes
- **Materials Needed**: copy of following page, scissors, plain paper, writing utensil, glue
- **How to Use**: Cut apart hamburgers and buns. Write helping ideas on the bottom of each bun and glue onto plain paper. When child helps without being asked, write name (for multiple children) or the date (for single child) on the top bun and have child glue the top bun to the bottom.
- **Additional Ideas**: Use for Scripture memory by writing verse on the top bun and reference on the bottom, mix them up and then match
- **Hint**: laminate and use Velcro to reuse another time
- **Educational Benefit**: sight words, matching parts
- **Optional Incentive**: have a hamburger cookout (and don't forget to help)

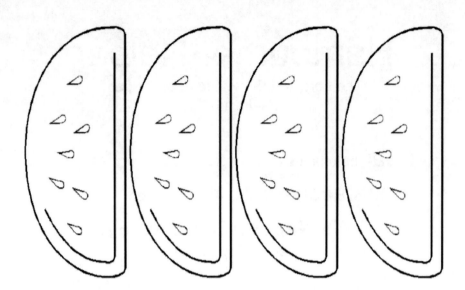

H A M B U R G E R
H E L P E R

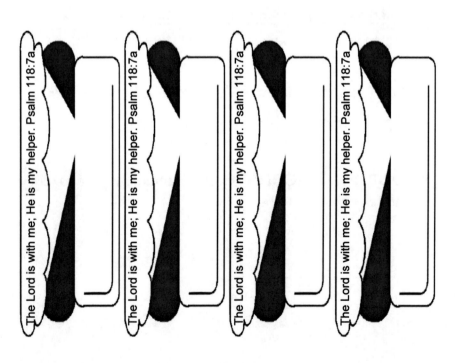

Happiness Hippo

"A cheerful heart is good medicine."
Proverbs 17:22a

- **Goal:** joyfulness
- **Preparation Time:** 0-5 minutes
- **Materials Needed:** copy of following page, crayons or stickers
- **How to Use:** Each time child shows joyfulness, color in (or place sticker on) a section of hippo's body until all sections are filled.
- **Additional Ideas:** use the same idea for other "h" words (Helping Hippo, Hardworking Hippo, Honest Hippo, etc.)
- **Hint:** shrink hippo to 2/page to use for different goals or for multiple children
- **Educational Benefit:** completing a chart, alliteration, letter sounds
- **Optional Incentive:** go outside and blow bubbles, play Hungry Hippo game

Heart of Wisdom

"Teach us to number our days aright,
that we may gain a heart of wisdom."
Psalm 90:12

- **Goal**: wise choices
- **Preparation Time**: 5-10 minutes
- **Materials Needed**: 2 large hearts, scissors, writing utensil, sticky tac
- **How to Use**: Divide both hearts into 6 identical sections. Label the 1st heart with one letter of "wisdom" in each section (do not cut apart). Label the 2nd heart with numbers 1-6 and cut apart. Attach the 2nd heart to top of the 1st heart with sticky tac. Each time wisdom is demonstrated (making good choices, using self-control, obeying, etc.), child may remove one numbered section of top heart until all letters of wisdom are revealed.
- **Additional Ideas**: see also Color by Number
- **Hint**: use a page from a coloring book and have child color one section at a time
- **Educational Benefit**: number and shape recognition, fine motor skills
- **Optional Incentive**: play hopscotch and stop to say a word from Psalm 90:12 in each square

Har-money

"Live in harmony with one another."
Romans 12:16a

- **Goal**: cooperation
- **Preparation Time**: 0-5 minutes
- **Materials Needed**: coins (real or fake), empty margarine tub with slot in lid (1/child)
- **How to Use**: As children work or play in harmony together, give them coins to put in their "bank".
- **Additional Ideas**: use chocolate coins that children may eat when demonstrating harmony
- **Hint**: divide earnings to teach monetary responsibility—spend (60%), save (30%), tithe (10%)
- **Educational Benefit**: monetary responsibility, coin recognition, counting, adding, subtracting, sorting, percentages, fractions
- **Optional Incentive**: go to a store and allow child to spend earnings

Heavenly Pair-a-Dice

"Those who are in the flesh cannot please God. You, however, are not in the flesh but in the Spirit, if in fact the Spirit of God dwells in you."
Romans 8:8-9a (ESV)

- **Goal**: behavior
- **Preparation Time**: 5-10 minutes
- **Materials Needed**: 2 dice, paper, writing utensil
- **How to Use**: Make a numbered list of 11 positive behaviors for child to work on. Roll dice and add together. The total rolled is the goal for the day (e.g. if you roll a 1 and 4, work on item 5).
- **Additional Ideas**: use the same way, but only list 6 behaviors and have child work on 2 things (e.g. items 1 *and* 4)
- **Hint**: discuss behaviors with child and create list together
- **Educational Benefit**: addition, reading, numbering and creating a list
- **Optional Incentive**: play a game involving dice (CLR, Bunko, Yahtzee, etc.)

Helping Hippo

"Pay attention to what I say; listen closely to my words."
Proverbs 4:20

- **Goal**: helpfulness
- **Preparation Time**: 5-10 minutes
- **Materials Needed**: 2 paper plates (cut one in half), copy of following page cut out, glue, writing utensil, slips of paper
- **How to Use**: Assemble paper plate hippo by gluing the half plate backwards to whole plate forming a pocket, then attaching helping hippo to the top. Each time child helps, write it down and put in the hippo pocket. When hippo is full (or predetermined number has been reached) reread all the ways the child has helped.
- **Additional Ideas**: Have various prewritten thank you notes inside hippo and when child helps, he draws a thank you note.
- **Hint**: For younger children, have prewritten helping ideas inside hippo that child pulls out.
- **Educational Benefit**: reading, following directions
- **Optional Incentive**: visit the hippos at the zoo, play Hungry Hippo game

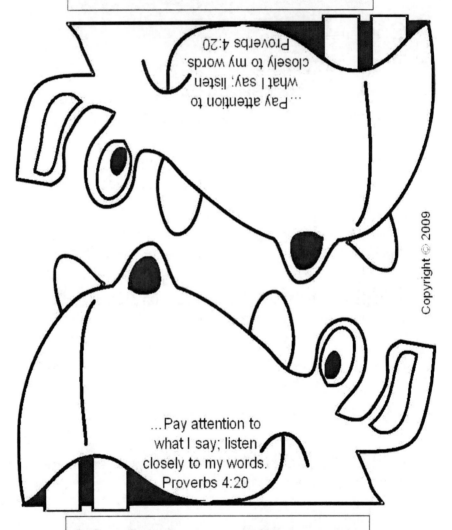

Hide & Seek-Ye-First

"…Seek first His kingdom and His righteousness…."
Matthew 6:33

- **Goal**: attitude (righteousness)
- **Preparation Time**: 10-20 minutes
- **Materials Needed**: slips of paper, writing utensil, several small treasures or one large treasure (see Hint)
- **How to Use**: Hide several objects around the house, then write clues to their whereabouts. When child demonstrates seeking the Lord (or showing an example of righteousness), give a clue that leads to one of the hidden treasures.
- **Additional Ideas**: use for sports, behavior, chores, etc.
- **Hint**: Have one special treasure and x-number of clues. Each time child demonstrates goal, give an additional clue toward finding the treasure.
- **Educational Benefit**: reading comprehension, logical reasoning
- **Optional Incentive**: let child make a treasure hunt for parent

Hmmm…Interesting

"Let each of you look not only to his own interests, but also to the interests of others."
Philippians 2:4 (ESV)

- **Goal**: thoughtfulness
- **Preparation Time**: 0-5 minutes initially (adult), 5-10 minutes daily (child)
- **Materials Needed**: notepad, drawing or writing utensil
- **How to Use**: Encourage child to find at least one interesting thing daily about another family member and record it in notepad. Be sure to put the date and the name and reason of the person of interest.
- **Additional Ideas**: divide a binder into sections with each child's name for multiple children
- **Hint**: Have younger children draw pictures and older children draw with more detail and write a caption, or write a sentence or paragraph if preferred.
- **Educational Benefit**: illustration, attention to detail, writing, listening
- **Optional Incentive**: play charades as a family

Home Sweet Home

"By *wisdom* a house is built, and through *understanding* it is established; through *knowledge* its rooms are filled with rare and beautiful treasures."
Proverbs 24:3-4

- **Goal**: Scripture application
- **Preparation Time**: 5-10 minutes
- **Materials Needed**: popsicle sticks, yarn, small craft gems, glue, shoebox or pizza lid
- **How to Use**: When child demonstrates an understanding of wisdom, give popsicle sticks to "build" the framework of a house in the cardboard lid. When understanding is demonstrated, give child yarn to "establish" rooms inside the popsicle stick house. Finally, when knowledge is demonstrated, child may "fill" each room with the gems.
- **Additional Ideas**: have child draw (1st-house, 2nd-rooms, 3rd-treasures) instead of using craft supplies
- **Hint**: For shorter application, child may completely finish each step (e.g. build entire house at once). For longer application, break each step into smaller parts (e.g. one popsicle stick each time wisdom is demonstrated).
- **Educational Benefit**: art
- **Optional Incentive**: visit model homes or watch a residential construction site

Honey, Honey

"Gracious words are a honeycomb,
sweet to the soul and healing to the bones."
Proverbs 16:24

- **Goal**: kindness
- **Preparation Time**: 0-5 minutes
- **Materials Needed**: small jar, Honeycomb cereal
- **How to Use**: Fill a small jar with Honeycomb cereal. Each time pleasant words are used (without being reminded), allow child to eat a piece of the cereal.
- **Additional Ideas**: print out a picture of a honeycomb and have child color in a cell (or glue on a piece of cereal) each time pleasant words are spoken
- **Hint**: for more than one child, encourage siblings to catch each other using pleasant words and give them both a piece of cereal
- **Educational Benefit**: science and math (explore how bees make honey and why the cells are hexagonal)
- **Optional Incentive**: purchase a honeycomb from a specialty food store and enjoy the sweet taste

Hot Stuff
Daniel 3

- **Goal**: obedience
- **Preparation Time**: 0-5 minutes
- **Materials Needed**: copy of following page, scissors, red crayon or marker
- **How to Use**: Read Daniel 3 about the young men who obeyed God and were literally "hot stuff". Cut out a thermometer and label with child's name or obedience goal. Each time child obeys color a section on the thermometer (starting at the bottom) until the thermometer is filled up.
- **Additional Ideas**: use red string or a paper clip to move up or down
- **Hint**: for multiple children cut out several thermometers and label each one with child's name or a specific obedience issue
- **Educational Benefit**: thermometer recognition, opposites, directions
- **Optional Incentive**: have a pool party or eat some ice cream on a hot day

Hot Stuff

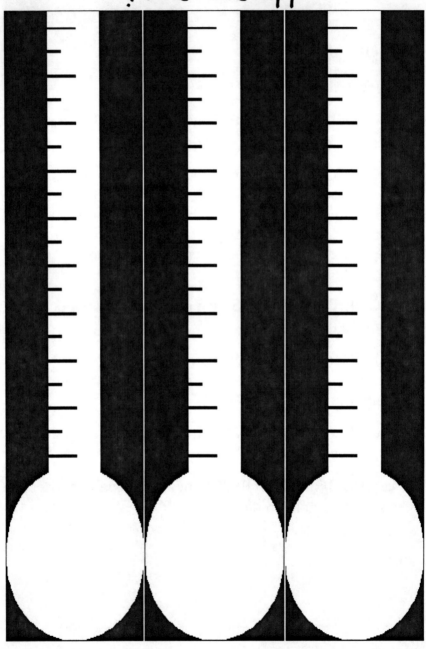

Humble Pie

"When pride comes, then comes disgrace,
but with humility comes wisdom."
Proverbs 11:2

- **Goal**: humility
- **Preparation Time**: 0-5 minutes
- **Materials Needed**: 2 cardboard circles, ruler, scissors, marker, sticky tac
- **How to Use**: Divide both circles into 8 equal sections. Write one letter of "HUMILITY" in each section of the 1st circle. Decorate the 2nd circle like a pie (optional) and cut out the pieces. Attach all 8 pieces onto 1st circle, covering every letter. Each time humility is demonstrated, child may remove a piece of Humble Pie until all 8 pieces have been "eaten" and the word HUMILITY is completely visible.
- **Additional Ideas:** start with empty pie and each time child demonstrates humility, write one letter (or what child did) on a piece and add to pie.
- **Hint**: recycle an aluminum pie pan or pizza box to form "pie"
- **Educational Benefit**: fractions, spelling
- **Optional Incentive**: celebrate completion of Humble Pie by having child's favorite pie and whipped cream for dessert that night

I Am Cape-Able

"God is our refuge and strength;
an ever-present help in trouble."
Psalm 46:1

- **Goal**: confidence
- **Preparation Time**: 0-5 minutes
- **Materials Needed**: empty cereal box, stickers (various shapes and sizes are fine), scissors
- **How to Use**: Cut cereal box into a trapezoid to resemble a cape. Each time confidence/capability is demonstrated, have child place a "patch" (sticker) on the "cape".
- **Additional Ideas**: make a cape out of an old towel and add real patches or scraps of material
- **Hint**: remind child that we can always ask God for strength, even when we don't feel courageous ourselves.
- **Educational Benefit**: counting, shapes
- **Optional Incentive**: watch a Larry Boy video (by the makers of Veggie Tales)

In Today's News...

"But encourage one another daily, as long as it is called 'Today,' so that none of you may be hardened by sin's deceitfulness."
Hebrews 3:13

- **Goal**: encouragement
- **Preparation Time**: 5-10 minutes daily with child
- **Materials Needed**: copy of following page (or an old unused calendar), glue, scissors (or writing utensil), newspaper
- **How to Use**: Post Today's News somewhere visible. At the end of each day, assist child (if needed) in finding an encouraging word or phrase from the newspaper to cut out and glue on the appropriate day. It can be about siblings, parents, friends, teachers, etc. or something encouraging from the day.
- **Additional Ideas**: if you don't receive the newspaper, save magazines or mailing ads, or just write encouraging words
- **Hint**: have children who don't yet read draw a picture or dictate what to write
- **Educational Benefit**: calendar skills, number recognition, sight words/reading
- **Optional Incentive**: save each month's news to make a complete calendar at the end of the year

IN TODAY'S NEWS...

1	2	3	4
5	6	7	8
9	10	11	12
13	14	15	16
17	18	19	20
21	22	23	24
25	26	27	28
29	30	31	"...encourage one another daily..." Hebrews 3:13

I Refuze!

"Do not follow the crowd in doing wrong."
Exodus 23:2a

- **Goal**: peer pressure
- **Preparation Time**: 0-5 minutes
- **Materials Needed**: fuze beads and board (found in craft section of stores), iron
- **How to Use**: Decide on either a predetermined number of fuze beads, or a certain design (e.g. cross, star, heart, etc.) for fuze board. Each time child demonstrates refusal to follow the crowd in doing wrong, give a fuze bead until predetermined number of beads have been received or child completes predetermined shape.
- **Additional Ideas**: purchase pre-shaped boards at craft store or on-line at Oriental Trading
- **Hint**: have child create fuze art, but be sure the *adult* fuses it together with the iron
- **Educational Benefit**: art
- **Optional Incentive**: create other fuze art projects with extra beads

J-O-Y Full

"I delight greatly in the Lord;
my soul rejoices in my God."
Isaiah 61:10a

- **Goal**: joyfulness
- **Preparation Time**: 0-5 minutes
- **Materials Needed**: empty 1 or 2-liter bottle (wrapping removed), heart with word J.O.Y. attached to the bottle, ¼ measuring cup, water, funnel, red food coloring (optional)
- **How to Use**: Before beginning, point to the word J.O.Y. on the bottle. Explain to child(ren) that true joy is only achieved when one puts Jesus first (J), then others (O), and yourself (Y) last. Then, each time child demonstrates joy, fill the bottle with ¼ cup of water and add 2-3 drops of red food coloring (if desired). Remove ¼ cup of water when child demonstrates the opposite of joy. Goal is to fill completely to overflowing (like our hearts should be when we're filled with the joy of the Lord).
- **Additional Ideas**: this is a fun visual idea for any behavior with opposites (obedience vs. disobedience, giving vs. taking, etc.)
- **Hint**: use more water each time to finish Booster quickly, less to keep it going longer
- **Educational Benefit**: measurement, opposites
- **Optional Incentive**: visit a malt shop and get an "overflowing" coke float

Joyful Jumping Jack

"A joyful heart is good medicine,
but a crushed spirit dries up the bones."
Proverbs 17:22 (ESV)

- **Goal**: joyfulness
- **Preparation Time**: 5-10 minutes
- **Materials Needed**: copy of following page (have child decorate one with different colors), scissors, glue, baggie
- **How to Use**: Cut apart each colored piece of Jack, and around just the outline of the plain one. When child demonstrates a joyful heart, write it on one piece of cut apart body and glue onto plain copy of Jack until Jack is complete (optional—remove a piece when not joyful).
- **Additional Ideas**: print onto cardstock and use brads to attach each section of body so Jack can jump for joy
- **Hint**: copy onto cardstock for endurance and use velcro to reuse, or for more than one child, put name of child demonstrating joy on the piece before child attaches
- **Educational Benefit**: matching parts
- **Optional Incentive**: do some joyful jumping jacks while repeating verse

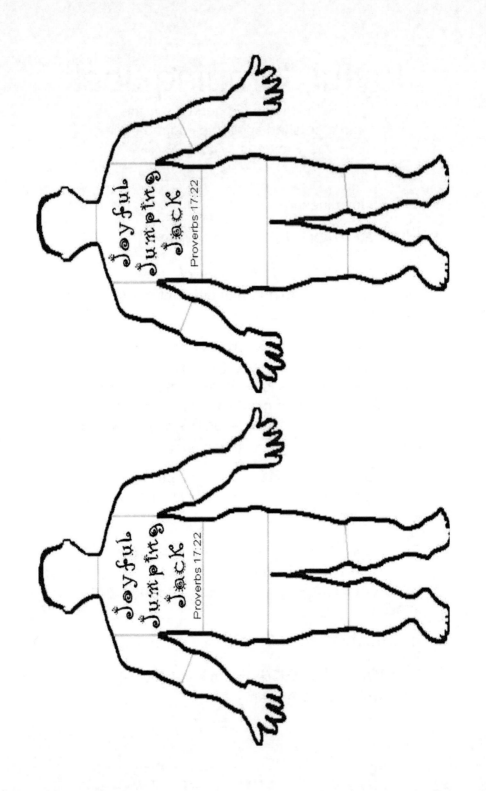

Keep Me in Stitches

"Then our mouth was filled with laughter,
and our tongue with shouts of joy."
Psalm 126:2a (ESV)

- **Goal**: joyfulness
- **Preparation Time**: 0-5 minutes
- **Materials Needed**: simple child's stitchery kit (found in craft stores, often in dollar section)
- **How to Use**: Child may add a stitch toward the final stitched picture each time a joyful attitude is demonstrated,
- **Additional Ideas**: for multiple children, each child can work on an individual stitchery kit, or they can each use the same one as a team project
- **Hint**: if one stitch at a time takes too long, allow a stitch for each joyful word used
- **Educational Benefit**: hand-eye coordination, fine motor skills, following directions
- **Optional Incentive**: when the stitched picture is complete, have child send it to someone special

Kinder Reminder

"Always strive to do what is good for each other and for everyone else."
1 Thessalonians 5:15b

- **Goal**: kindness / love
- **Preparation Time**: 5-10 minutes
- **Materials Needed**: empty tissue box, wrapping paper (optional), writing utensil, small note paper
- **How to Use**: Wrap tissue box and label "Kinder Reminder". Then have child share some examples of kindness, write them down, and put into the tissue box. When having difficulty being kind, have child pull out a Kinder Reminder and do what it says.
- **Additional Ideas**: have children come up with kind things they can do for each other
- **Hint**: if old enough, encourage children to write the Kinder Reminders on their own to solidify their thoughts
- **Educational Benefit**: writing, reading, spelling, comprehension
- **Optional Incentive**: let child think of ways to be kind to strangers and do them as a family (e.g. nursing home, soup kitchen)

Knight in Shining Armor

"Put on the full armor of God, so that you can take your stand against the devil's schemes."
Ephesians 6:11

- **Goal**: Scripture application
- **Preparation Time**: 0-5 minutes
- **Materials Needed**: picture of a knight (should have *helmet, sword, breastplate, shield, belt, footwear)
- **How to Use**: As understanding & application is demonstrated from each characteristic of Ephesians 6:14-17* (see below), child may color in that piece of the armor.
- **Additional Ideas**: Take full length picture of child. Cut out armor (see Materials Needed). Dress "knight" (see How to Use).
- **Hint**: have child cut pieces out of aluminum foil to make shiny, metallic armor
- **Educational Benefit**: recognizing and naming parts of armor, spelling--silent "k" in knight (knife, knee, know, etc.)
- **Optional Incentive**: visit a museum or castle to observe real armor

---

*Read Ephesians 6:14-17

Belt - Truth
Shield - Faith
Helmet - Salvation
Sword - Spirit (God's Word)
Breastplate - Righteousness
Footwear - Peace, Readiness

Last Place

"So the last will be first, and the first will be last."
Matthew 20:16

- **Goal**: thoughtfulness / patience
- **Preparation Time**: 0-5 minutes
- **Materials Needed**: 1st place ribbon (found in craft or sports stores), marker
- **How to Use**: Use marker to change "1st" to "last" on ribbon. Each time patience or thoughtfulness (e.g. being the last to receive dessert, waiting patiently for the bathroom, waiting to talk until parent is off the phone, etc.) is demonstrated, give child the "last place" ribbon to wear.
- **Additional Ideas**: create a race track, start at the finish line, and go backwards (toward last place)
- **Hint**: the goal for multiple children is to get in the habit of being last (i.e. patient and thoughtful) so a fun way to practice is with the incentive to be the one wearing the Last Place ribbon
- **Educational Benefit**: opposites
- **Optional Incentive**: go to the park and take turns being *last* on the swing, slide, etc.

Listening Lips

"…Be quick to listen, slow to speak, and slow to become angry."
James 1:19b

- **Goal**: patience (listening skills)
- **Preparation Time**: 5-10 minutes
- **Materials Needed**: copy of following page (child may color), empty jar, scissors
- **How to Use**: Cut out ears and lips. Place *ears* in the jar when child is being a good listener, *lips* in the jar when child is too quick to speak (e.g. interrupting, arguing). Goal is to have all the ears in the jar before the lips.
- **Additional Ideas**: For multiple children, write name on back of lips and ears before placing in jar (be sure to praise improvement and discreetly encourage whomever needs more practice listening).
- **Hint**: use on a regular basis for best results
- **Educational Benefit**: sorting, counting, more than/less than
- **Optional Incentive**: go to local library for story time (and be a good listener)

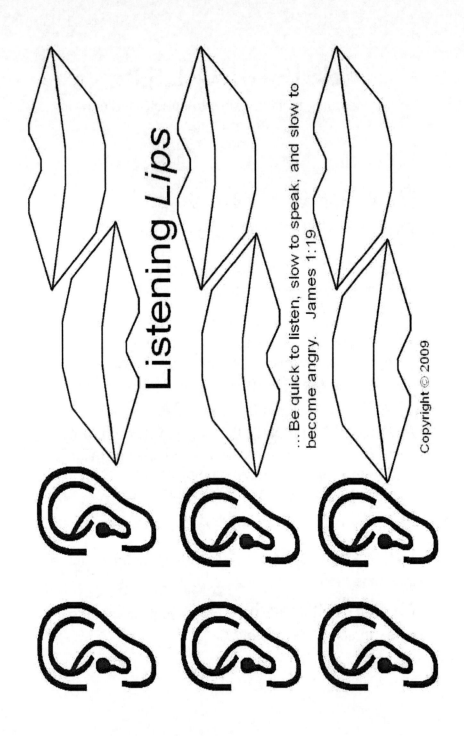

Love One AnUdder

"Let us love one another, for love comes from God."
1 John 4:7a

- **Goal**: love
- **Preparation Time**: 5-10 minutes
- **Materials Needed**: copy of following page on cardstock, glue, black felt, scissors
- **How to Use**: Cut felt into the same shapes as the spots on the cow. Each time love is demonstrated (verbally, physically, etc.), allow child to glue a felt "spot" onto the cow.
- **Additional Ideas**: cut out spots from a brown paper bag to glue on, and write the example of love shown on each spot (or for multiple children using the same cow, write the name of who showed love to whom)
- **Hint**: recycle what you already have by using popsicle sticks and a toilet paper roll to make a cow, then make "spots" with cotton balls
- **Educational Benefit**: matching shapes, agriculture (explore which cows have spots, the purpose of an udder, etc.)
- **Optional Incentive**: visit a farm or petting zoo (and perhaps even milk a cow)

Love Reporter

"Since God so loved us,
we also ought to love one another."
1 John 4:11

- **Goal**: love
- **Preparation Time**: 5-10 minutes
- **Materials Needed**: 30 or so hearts cut from red or pink paper (or several copies of following page and scissors), writing utensil, tape
- **How to Use**: When child demonstrates love, write that example shown on a heart (e.g. talked to visitor at church, shared snack with someone who didn't have one, helped sibling up after falling, etc.). Tape hearts to the wall to spell out the word LOVE.
- **Additional Ideas**: Encourage children to be love reporters on siblings, other family members, or friends who show acts of love
- **Hint**: to make multiple hearts at once, fold paper into fourths or sixths, outline one heart, cut through the folds
- **Educational Benefit**: writing/reading sentences
- **Optional Incentive**: have fun with some heart cookie cutters and play dough

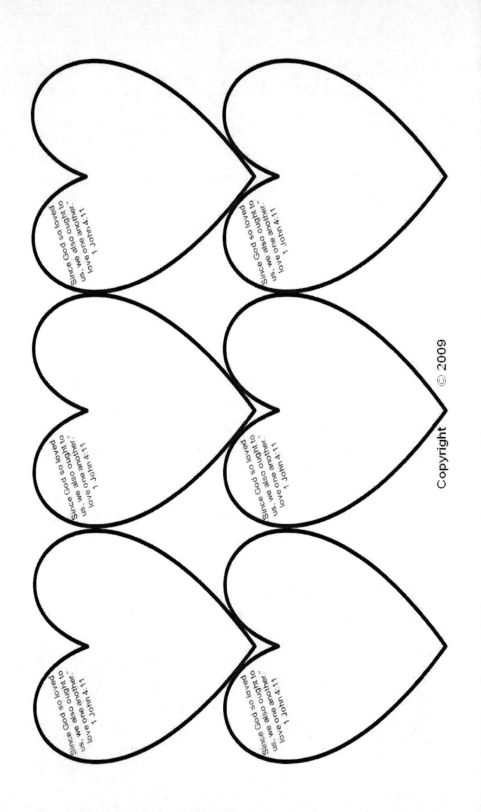

Love Links
1 Corinthians 13:4-8a

- **Goal**: love / Scripture application
- **Preparation Time**: 5-10 minutes
- **Materials Needed**: Bible, 16 strips of pink paper, stapler, writing utensil
- **How to Use**: Read above Bible passage together, then write a different love application on each strip. As child demonstrates understanding of one, shape into a heart and staple, gradually linking hearts together.
- **Additional Ideas**: use heart cut-outs and a hole punch, then link together with yarn
- **Hint**: write child's name and example of the love he/she demonstrated on back of link before attaching
- **Educational Benefit**: motor skills (shaping and connecting strips)
- **Optional Incentive**: link some Fruit by the Foot together as a fun snack

M & M's

"Let us therefore make every effort to do what leads to peace and to mutual edification."
Romans 14:19

- **Goal**: thoughtfulness
- **Preparation Time**: 0-5 minutes
- **Materials Needed**: small jar, M&M candies
- **How to Use**: Write child's name on the jar and fill with M&M's. When child demonstrates good manners (please, thank-you, sharing, kind voice, etc.) or meekness (humility, gentleness, etc.) give a piece of candy.
- **Additional Ideas**: for more than one child, have separate jars or use one for when they show manners and/or meekness with one another
- **Hint**: a baby food jar will fit over 100 regular M&M's
- **Educational Benefit**: counting, vocabulary (meekness), letter sounds (m)
- **Optional Incentive**: use left-over candies to make M&M cookies together

Maker's Doesen

"Even a child makes himself known by his acts,
by whether his conduct is pure and upright."
Proverbs 20:11 (ESV)

- **Goal**: self-initiative / thoughtfulness
- **Preparation Time**: 15-20 minutes
- **Materials Needed**: 13 brown circles (with smaller circle cut out of center like a donut), crayon shavings (or glitter), plate, writing utensil, glue
- **How to Use**: When child does something without being told, write it on a brown "donut" and have child "frost" with crayon shavings or glitter. Glue each one onto the plate until there is a Baker's Dozen…uh…Maker's Doesen.
- **Additional Ideas**: Pre-make 13 "donuts" with reward written on back and let child choose one each time he/she does something without being told.
- **Hint**: if using crayon shavings, put donut between 2 pieces of wax paper and iron on low
- **Educational Benefit**: art, counting
- **Optional Incentive**: have donuts for breakfast or dessert

Manner Marks

"Show proper respect to everyone, love the family of believers, fear God…"
1 Peter 2:17

- **Goal**: respect
- **Preparation Time**: 0-5 minutes
- **Materials Needed**: paper, writing utensil
- **How to Use**: Divide paper into sections depending on how many children will work on manners. Each time manners are demonstrated, allow child to draw a tally mark on his section.
- **Additional Ideas**: glue toothpicks on cardboard to keep tally marks
- **Hint**: Allow siblings to give each other permission to get a tally mark when they notice good manners.
- **Educational Benefit**: basic math
- **Optional Incentive**: enjoy a shake at Chick-fil-A while tallying how many times good manners are used by their employees

Map Quest

"Search me, O God, and know my heart...see if there is any offensive way in me, and lead me in the way everlasting."
Psalm 139:23-24

- **Goal**: behavior (righteousness)
- **Preparation Time**: 5-10 minutes
- **Materials Needed**: plain paper, writing utensil
- **How to Use**: Write child's name and street (e.g. Lexi Ln., Cody Ct.) at the top left corner of the paper, and "Everlasting Way" at the bottom right. Each time child demonstrates righteousness, draw a line on the paper and write what it was on the line. The next time draw a line going a different way (like a map), and so on until "Everlasting Way" is reached.
- **Additional Ideas**: print out a maze and have child draw a line toward the finish each time righteousness is demonstrated
- **Hint**: draw more or fewer lines depending on child's age and understanding
- **Educational Benefit**: map familiarization
- **Optional Incentive**: dine at child's favorite restaurant, but have child give the directions on how the get there (this could take a while, but encourage them to ask for help if confused or lost, just as we ask our Heavenly Father for guidance)

Marbleous Jar

"Don't let anyone look down on you because you are young, but set an example for the believers in speech, in life, in love, in faith, and in purity."
1 Timothy 4:12

- **Goal**: "marvelous" behavior
- **Preparation Time**: 0-5 minutes
- **Materials Needed**: small jar, marbles
- **How to Use**: Each time child is behaving marvelously, place a marble in a jar (and/or remove marble when child is misbehaving). When jar is filled, goal is reached.
- **Additional Ideas**: use for schoolwork, teamwork, chores, sportsmanship, etc.
- **Hint**: a baby food jar takes 30-50 marbles to fill, so this is a long-term accomplishment
- **Educational Benefit**: counting, estimating
- **Optional Incentive**: let child choose special "date" with parent

Master Blaster

"No one can serve two masters. Either you will hate the one and love the other, or you will be devoted to the one and despise the other."
Matthew 6:24

- **Goal**: behavior
- **Preparation Time**: 5-10 minutes
- **Materials Needed**: copy of following page (have child color), yarn, ruler, paper clip, scissors
- **How to Use**: Cut out the rockets, circle, cloud, and one foot of yarn, marking at every inch. You will need: [1]rocket labeled with child's name, [2]cloud labeled with desired (heavenly) behavior, [3]circle labeled with opposite (earthly) behavior. Tape the circle to bottom of yarn and cloud to the top. Clip the rocket to bottom of yarn at earthly behavior and "blast" upward each time child demonstrates heavenly behavior, or down for earthly behavior, until child has "mastered" heavenly behavior.
- **Additional Ideas**: use several rockets labeled with behaviors needing improvement, and see which behavior shows most/least improvement
- **Hint**: glue rocket onto cardboard for durability
- **Educational Benefit**: directions (up and down)
- **Optional Incentive**: celebrate with sparkler fireworks, or go to local airport and watch planes take off

Money Talk$

"One who loves a pure heart and who speaks with grace will have the king for a friend."
Proverbs 22:11

- **Goal**: tone of voice / kindness
- **Preparation Time**: 0-5 minutes
- **Materials Needed**: pretend money (bills in denominations of at least five 1's, one 5, one 10), inexpensive "prizes"
- **How to Use**: Each time child uses his voice or words kindly, "pay" child $1 in pretend money. When child uses his voice to be unkind, child should pay you $1. Goal is for child to earn $10 in pretend money to "buy" a prize.
- **Additional Ideas**: use bills from Monopoly or Life games, make some with construction paper, or look for some at a dollar or teacher store
- **Hint**: This Booster can be used year-round. If $10 is taking too long to achieve (or child is younger) adjust the goal to a lower amount, and vice versa.
- **Educational Benefit**: adding, subtracting, number sense and recognition, opposites
- **Optional Incentive**: play a Monopoly or Life board game as a family

Mouth Trap

"Evildoers are trapped by their sinful talk,
…the innocent escape trouble."
Proverbs 12:13

- **Goal**: attitude / tone of voice
- **Preparation Time**: 0-5 minutes
- **Materials Needed**: mousetrap (<u>spring removed</u> so it won't snap shut), wax candy lips
- **How to Use**: Place lips next to the mousetrap. If child uses sinful talk (arguing, unkind tone, bad words, etc.), place lips in the mouse trap. When child uses kind words or tone, remove the lips. At the end of the day, if lips are not on the mouse trap, allow child to have the candy lips.
- **Additional Ideas**: Cut out a person shape in place of wax lips and use the same way. Goal is to have "righteous" man all the way out, therefore escaping trouble.
- **Hint**: make sure you have completely disabled the mousetrap and keep out of reach of children
- **Educational Benefit**: opposites (in/out, trapped/escaped)
- **Optional Incentive**: play "Mousetrap" game by Hasbro

Muscle Man

"It is God who arms me with strength
and keeps my way secure."
Psalm 18:32

- **Goal**: increase positive behavior
- **Preparation Time**: 0-5 minutes
- **Materials Needed**: copy of following page, red crayon
- **How to Use**: Write behavior goal on bicep. Each time child demonstrates behavior goal, color in a "muscle" from the smallest bump upward, to show how the more we rely on God when we're having trouble, the stronger we become, because God is our strength.
- **Additional Ideas**: Cut out several pictures of a muscle man. Determine a behavior goal and write one letter on each muscle man. Each time child demonstrates behavior goal, add one muscle man to the next, forming a chain of muscle men until the behavior goal is spelled out.
- **Hint**: Have child try to lift something heavy, then have them lift it again with adult help. Explain to child that sometimes burdens are too heavy to lift alone, and it's okay to ask for help.
- **Educational Benefit**: science (human body)
- **Optional Incentive**: have a push-up contest and feel those biceps at work

Music Machine

"Make a joyful noise unto the Lord, all the earth!"
Psalm 100:1 (ESV)

- **Goal**: joyfulness
- **Preparation Time**: 0-5 minutes
- **Materials Needed**: copy of following page (xylophone), crayons (or colored craft sticks and glue)
- **How to Use**: When child demonstrates joyfulness, write it on a bar on a xylophone bar and color. Goal is to color all 8 xylophone bars in a timely manner. Or write 8 examples of joyfulness on colored craft sticks. As child demonstrates one, glue it onto xylophone bar.
- **Additional Ideas**: Use music notes instead of xylophone. Wrap shoe box and cut a slit on top. Each time child demonstrates joy, write it on a music note and put in box. When needing encouragement, take out music notes and read.
- **Hint**: if using craft sticks, look for colored ones at dollar store or craft shop
- **Educational Benefit**: recognize colors and musical instruments
- **Optional Incentive**: "play" completed xylophone using a lollipop as the striker

Music Machine

Make a joyful noise unto the Lord, all the earth!
Psalm 100:1 (ESV)

The No Whine Vine

"I am the Vine, you are the branches. If you remain in Me and I in you, you will bear much fruit. Apart from me, you can do nothing."
John 15:5

- **Goal**: tone of voice / attitude
- **Preparation Time**: 5-10 minutes
- **Materials Needed**: copy of following page, purple or green washable stamp pad (or marker)
- **How to Use**: Place the grape bunch in a visible location. Help child stamp a thumbprint onto one grape each time child chooses to demonstrate a positive attitude instead of whining. Goal is reached when all grapes have a thumbprint.
- **Additional Ideas**: Punch a hole in the outer grapes and thread a long piece of yarn through, one grape at a time, whenever positive attitude is demonstrated until yarn has gone through the entire grapevine (optional--remove one each time child whines).
- **Hint**: write date of positive attitude on grapes
- **Educational Benefit**: fine motor skills
- **Optional Incentive**: go to a farm and pick grapes, or go on a picnic (don't forget the grapes!)

The No Whine

I'm the Vine, you are the branches. If you remain in Me and I in you, you will bear much fruit. Apart from me, you can do nothing.
John 15:5

Opossum Opposites

"How can a young person stay on the path of purity?
By living according to your word."
Psalm 119:9

- **Goal**: behavior
- **Preparation Time**: 5-10 minutes
- **Materials Needed**: hanger (or taught string), copy of following page on cardstock, scissors, writing utensil
- **How to Use**: Set specific behavior goal and its opposite (e.g. fighting & cooperation) and label ends of hanger. Cut out an opossum, write child's name on it, hang by tail onto hanger. Have child slide to appropriate side depending on behavior. Goal is to be on the positive behavior side.
- **Additional Ideas**: use a different hanger for each behavior issue, or use + and – signs and make marks along hanger for child to move a little at a time
- **Hint**: for multiple children using the same one, hanger and 'possum tails will probably need to be stabilized (attach small weights to either end)
- **Educational Benefit**: opposites, science (explore why opossums hang upside down and other nocturnal animals)
- **Optional Incentive**: go to a playground and hang upside down on the monkey bars like an opossum (with a supervising adult)

Opossum Opposites

How can a young person stay on the path of purity?
By living according to your word.
Psalm 119:9

Ought-to-Dot

"If anyone, then, knows the good they ought to do and doesn't do it, it is sin for them."
James 4:17

- **Goal**: responsibility
- **Preparation Time**: 0-5 minutes
- **Materials Needed**: dot-to-dot picture, writing utensil (or hole punch and string)
- **How to Use**: Have child choose a dot-to-dot picture and display in a visible location. Determine responsibility or behavior goal. Each time child demonstrates what he "ought to", have child connect one set of dots. Goal is to complete the Ought-to-Dot in a timely manner.
- **Additional Ideas**: instead of drawing lines, punch holes in a picture and have child put a string through each hole
- **Hint**: use fewer dots for younger children and more dots for older
- **Educational Benefit**: counting, fine motor skills
- **Optional Incentive**: use finger paints to color Ought-to-Dot when all dots are connected

Patient Prince(ss)

"Be patient with everyone."
1 Thessalonians 5:14b

- **Goal**: patience
- **Preparation Time**: 5-10 minutes
- **Materials Needed**: 2 identical pictures of a prince or princess (copied or glued onto cardstock), Ziploc bag, scissors, glue
- **How to Use**: Cut apart one copy of prince or princess like a puzzle and keep in bag. Place the second copy in a visible location. Each time patience is demonstrated, child may withdraw one puzzle piece from the bag and glue onto displayed picture until puzzle is complete.
- **Additional Ideas**: Make a blank crown with 7 tips. Each time child demonstrates patience, write a letter on one tip until the word "patient" is complete. Then child can decorate and wear.
- **Hint**: cut out smaller pieces for older children, larger pieces for younger children
- **Educational Benefit**: identifying matches
- **Optional Incentive**: celebrate at Burger *King* or Dairy *Queen*

Pearly Gates

"...How awesome is this place! This is none other than the house of God; this is the gate of heaven."
Genesis 28:17

- **Goal**: wise choices
- **Preparation Time**: 5-10 minutes
- **Materials Needed**: pipe cleaners (gold if available), pearls with holes (or white beads)
- **How to Use**: Connect pipe cleaners to resemble a gate (e.g. space 5 evenly upright, fold each top slightly over one going across, and fold each bottom over one laying across the bottom). Each time child demonstrates making a wise choice, unfold one pipe cleaner and insert a pearl to make a "pearly gate".
- **Additional Ideas**: for multiple children use one pipe cleaner per child or make a "gate" for each of them
- **Hint**: for a reachable goal, set a certain number of pearls to add per pipe cleaner per week
- **Educational Benefit**: counting, colors
- **Optional Incentive**: have child save the beads upon completion to make a piece of jewelry for someone special

Penny for Your Talks

"Before a word is on my tongue
you, Lord, know it completely."
Psalm 139:4

- **Goal**: tone of voice
- **Preparation Time**: 0-5 minutes
- **Materials Needed**: pennies, bag or bank
- **How to Use**: Each time child chooses to talk using kind words or a gentle tone, give a penny. Pennies may be used to "buy" something at the end of the day or week or designated amount of time.
- **Additional Ideas**: see also Attitude Adjustors
- **Hint**: Pennies may be used to "buy" computer time, a later bedtime, extra playtime, get of chores, etc. Doesn't need to be something tangible.
- **Educational Benefit**: counting, monetary differentiation & value
- **Optional Incentive**: put the paid pennies into a baby bottle and donate to a pregnancy resource center when bottle is full

Picture Prayers

"Therefore…pray for each other…"
James 5:16a

- **Goal**: prayer
- **Preparation Time**: 0-5 minutes
- **Materials Needed**: pictures of friends, small photo album (1 photo/page) or sketch book (see additional ideas)
- **How to Use**: Place pictures in a special album set aside just for prayer time. Each night have child turn to a picture pray for that family.
- **Additional Ideas**: If praying for one family each week, contact that family and ask them for specific prayer requests or praises. Create a journal by gluing family picture on individual pages in a sketch book and write requests for that family (write date in order to look back and see how God answered prayers).
- **Hint**: save pictures from Christmas letters to rotate through
- **Educational Benefit**: verbalizing formed thoughts, journal entry
- **Optional Incentive**: Allow child to call, send an email, or write letter to the family telling them about the prayer(s).

Power of Love

"And he has given us this command: Anyone who loves God must also love their brother and sister."
1 John 4:21

- **Goal**: love
- **Preparation Time**: 5-10 minutes
- **Materials Needed**: paper towel tube, scissors or exacto knife, outlet plugs, marker
- **How to Use**: Bend paper towel tube to make a power strip (one set/child) and draw circles with lines to resemble outlets. Cut slits in each "outlet". Remind children that not only has God given us the *power* to love each other (even when we don't feel like it), He has *commanded* us to love one another. Each time child follows God's command by demonstrating love, add an outlet plug to child's power strip.
- **Additional Ideas**: Create 7 outlets on power strip and label one plug for each day of the week. When child has done a good job showing love, plug in that days' cover onto the strip. If child had difficulty, must wait until the next week to cover that outlet. Goal is to cover all outlets in a week.
- **Hint**: for teamwork, use one power strip, or have children put plugs on other siblings strip
- **Educational Benefit**: science (electricity)
- **Optional Incentive**: choose a fun night light to purchase for room

Popcorn Praise

"Praise the Lord. How good it is to sing praises to our God, how pleasant and fitting to praise him!"
Psalm 147:1

- **Goal**: prayer (praise)
- **Preparation Time**: 0-5 minutes
- **Materials Needed**: unused popcorn bag, scissors, yellow paper, writing utensil
- **How to Use**: Cut out popcorn shapes from yellow paper. Each time the opportunity arises, write praises on the popcorn, including positive observations of other family members. Say a short prayer aloud and place in bag (or place in bag and wait to pray until family prayer time).
- **Additional Ideas**: Have children think of at least one praise each day to put into bag before bed, then review in prayer weekly.
- **Hint**: in a family setting, take turns "popping" your praises out loud to get comfortable talking to God in front of others
- **Educational Benefit**: writing/reading sentences
- **Optional Incentive**: enjoy some popcorn with the family

Pure Nonsense

"…Whatever is *true*, whatever is *noble*, whatever is *right*, whatever is *pure*, whatever is *lovely*, whatever is *admirable*… think about such things."
Philippians 4:8

- **Goal**: Scripture application
- **Preparation Time**: 5-10 minutes
- **Materials Needed**: copy of following page, small post-it note, writing utensil
- **How to Use**: Write child's name on post-it note and place on the trash can. Each time child chooses to think/act on things listed above (see italicized words from verse), move toward purity. Move toward nonsense when child chooses to do what is opposite of Philippians 4:8 (optional).
- **Additional Ideas**: write an italicized word from Phil. 4:8 on each post-it note and stick on either purity or nonsense when child demonstrates applicable adjectives
- **Hint**: for multiple children use one line for each (there are 3/pg)
- **Educational Benefit**: opposites, adjective vocabulary
- **Optional Incentive**: have fun taking out the trash together and make a point of throwing it out (much like we should throw out the trash in our minds so that our thoughts can be pure)

"…Whatever is *true*, whatever is *noble*, whatever is *right*, whatever is *pure*, whatever is *lovely*, whatever is *admirable*… think about such things."
Philippians 4:8

Put a Cork in It

"Do not lie to each other."
Colossians 3:9a

- **Goal**: honesty
- **Preparation Time**: 0-5 minutes
- **Materials Needed**: plate, marker(s), corks, glue
- **How to Use**: Draw a happy face on a plate, making the smile extra large (like a semi-circle). Each time child demonstrates honesty attach cork to the smile. Goal is to fill mouth with corks.
- **Additional Ideas**: use large corks and write one letter on each cork as it is put in mouth until "honesty" is spelled out
- **Hint**: use different size corks depending on how long you desire to work on honesty (smaller corks will take longer)
- **Educational Benefit**: spelling, art, texture
- **Optional Incentive**: let child play with extra corks (stack to make tower, attach together to form art, use for Respecter Gadget, etc.)

Puzzle Peace

"Hold them in the highest regard in love because of their work. Live in peace with each other."
1 Thessalonians 5:13

- **Goal**: peace
- **Preparation Time**: 0-5 minutes
- **Materials Needed**: jigsaw puzzle (larger and fewer pieces for younger children, smaller and more pieces for older children), roll-up puzzle keeper (optional)
- **How to Use**: Each time child chooses to demonstrate peace in a seemingly tough situation, give a piece to add to the puzzle until puzzle is complete. Assemble puzzle on a roll-up puzzle keeper to easily move out of the way as needed (optional).
- **Additional Ideas**: enlarge a photo of child/family and cut into puzzle pieces
- **Hint**: use one puzzle for the entire family, or a separate puzzle for each child
- **Educational Benefit**: hand-eye coordination, photography
- **Optional Incentive**: complete a 3-D puzzle together as a family

Quick Sand

"Whoever is patient has great understanding,
but one who is quick-tempered displays folly."
Proverbs 14:29

- **Goal**: patience
- **Preparation Time**: 5-10 minutes
- **Materials Needed**: 2 colors of sand (e.g. blue and red), 2 baggies, clear jar, a tablespoon measuring tool
- **How to Use**: Place sand in two separate baggies and designate one color as patience and the other as quick-tempered. When patience is demonstrated, allow child to place one tablespoon of sand into the jar. When a quick-temper is shown, place one tablespoon of opposite color into the jar. Continue until jar is full and note which color was put in more frequently (ideally the patience color). Empty and try it again, this time achieving even more patient sand.
- **Additional Ideas**: Fill jar with sand and remove 1 tbs. each time child shows impatience. Goal is to have sand remaining (showing patience) at the end of set time.
- **Hint**: sand options: 1.play sand 2.sugar filled candy straws 3.salt & pepper 4.moon sand
- **Educational Benefit**: colors, art, measurement
- **Optional Incentive**: make some sand art (find at most craft stores) or build a sand-castle

Rainbow of _____
(Fill in the blank)

"I've set my rainbow in the clouds and it will be the sign of covenant between me and the earth."
Genesis 9:13

- **Goal**: behavior
- **Preparation Time**: 0-5 minutes
- **Materials Needed**: wax paper, multi-colored string (licorice-style) candy or Wikki Sticks, marker
- **How to Use**: Write a behavior goal at the bottom of wax paper strip. As child demonstrates the goal, place a colored candy string in a curve to form the first color of a rainbow. Repeat 6 times (or predetermined number) until rainbow is formed.
- **Additional Ideas**: Draw one rainbow and write 7 different goals to achieve (one goal per color). Color in one stripe each time child achieves goal, until rainbow is complete.
- **Hint**: place another piece of wax paper on top to keep candy rainbow from drying out
- **Educational Benefit**: art, science, colors
- **Optional Incentive**: depending on material used, child may eat or play with rainbow upon completion

Red Hot Obedience Pot

"Children, obey your parents in the Lord,
for this is right."
Ephesians 6:1

- **Goal**: obedience
- **Preparation Time**: 0-5 minutes
- **Materials Needed**: small jar, red hot candies
- **How to Use**: Fill the jar with red hot candies. When child obeys *immediately*, give a piece of red hot candy.
- **Additional Ideas**: Give one candy for obeying immediately and two candies for obeying immediately and acknowledging they heard you (e.g. saying "yes, Ma'am" or "yes, Sir", or repeating what you told them).
- **Hint**: over 100 red hot candies will fill a baby food jar
- **Educational Benefit**: understanding metaphors (red hot=quickly), counting
- **Optional Incentive**: play Red Light, Green Light which requires obedience, listening, and self-control skills

Red Light, Green Light

"God is our refuge and strength,
an ever-present help in trouble."
Psalm 46:1

- **Goal**: behavior
- **Preparation Time**: 5-10 minutes
- **Materials Needed**: use construction paper (red, green, and yellow cut in circles, and black) to create a stoplight, clothespins, writing utensil
- **How to Use**: Write behavior goal at the top of the stoplight (or write one goal on each clothespin). Label the green light with a positive consequence and the red light with a negative consequence. Start each day with the clothespin(s) attached to the green light. Move back and forth as necessary, but follow through on the consequence depending on which color child is on at the end of the day (or predetermined amount of time).
- **Additional Ideas**: write name on clothespins for multiple children working on same behavior
- **Hint**: laminate stoplight to reuse, and use vis-à-vis to write behaviors
- **Educational Benefit**: colors, direction (up/down), street sense
- **Optional Incentive**: have some friends over to play the "Red Light, Green Light" game outside

Responsibility Chart

"…Those who plan what is good
find love and faithfulness."
Proverbs 14:22b

- **Goal**: responsibility
- **Preparation Time**: 0-5 minutes
- **Materials Needed**: copy of following page, stickers, writing utensil
- **How to Use**: Fill in the chart with age-appropriate responsibilities. Set a weekly goal (e.g. earn 4 stickers/day for at least 5 days) to achieve incentive. Before bed each night, have child place a sticker next to each responsibility accomplished.
- **Additional Ideas**: use for behavior or Scripture memory
- **Hint**: as a general rule, give child 2 responsibilities per year of age (e.g. if child is 4, give 8 responsibilities)
- **Educational Benefit**: charting, plotting, reading a graph
- **Optional Incentive**: give child some money and let child demonstrate responsibility by purchasing a reward (toy, food, stickers, etc.)

Responsibility Chart

____ stickers/day for at least ____ days = _____ (goal)

Those who plan what is good find love and faithfulness. Proverbs 14:22b	SUN	MON	TUES	WED	THU	FRI	SAT

Ruler of All

"Direct my footsteps according to your word;
let no sin rule over me."
Psalm 119:133

- **Goal**: obedience
- **Preparation Time**: 0-5 minutes
- **Materials Needed**: copy of following page, markers or paper clip, scissors (optional)
- **How to Use**: Cut out one ruler (per child or per behavior). Each time child obeys and does not let sin rule, color an inch or use paper clips on the ruler. Go up the ruler for obedience and down for disobedience (if using paperclips) until the top of the ruler is reached.
- **Additional Ideas**: use an actual ruler and a binder clip to move up and down (or buy a tape measure at a dollar store)
- **Hint**: for multiple children, cut out several rulers and label each one with child's name or a specific obedience issue
- **Educational Benefit**: number recognition, opposites, directions
- **Optional Incentive**: Be king/queen for the day; get a crown from Burger King and celebrate ruling over/conquering the "kingdom of disobedience".

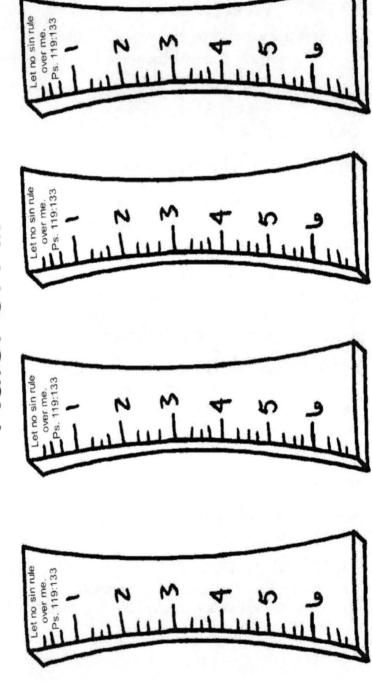

Respecter Gadget

"Whoever scorns instruction will pay for it,
but whoever respects a command is rewarded."
Proverbs 13:13

- **Goal**: respect / obedience
- **Preparation Time**: 5-10 minutes
- **Materials Needed**: springs x4, corks x4, Styrofoam cone and sphere, buttons x5, markers (or see Hint)
- **How to Use**: Child will be constructing his/her own robot-style creation called "Respecter Gadget". Each time child chooses to respect a command (obey), give one item for child to add toward its completion. Optional—remove a gadget when child disobeys or disrespects a command.
- **Additional Ideas**: using a sheet of paper and a drawing utensil, have child draw one part of the "Respecter Gadget" each time respect/obedience is demonstrated
- **Hint**: allow child to choose and use recycled household items to build the "Respecter Gadget"
- **Educational Benefit**: recycling, shapes, construction
- **Optional Incentive**: visit a children's science museum

Salt & Light

"You are the salt of the earth…You are the light of the world…Let your light shine before others, that they may see your good deeds and glorify your Father in heaven."
Matthew 5:13-16

- **Goal**: thoughtfulness
- **Preparation Time**: 5-10 minutes
- **Materials Needed**: black paper, glue, salt, star shape, white crayon
- **How to Use**: Trace several stars on the black paper. As child demonstrates being a light (good deeds), use glue and salt ("of the earth") to fill a star. Soon the darkness of the paper will become lighter with all the stars "shining".
- **Additional Ideas**: Instead of using salt and stars, use a whole-punch on the black paper and note how the light shines through more and more as additional holes are punched.
- **Hint**: reuse the salt that doesn't stick to stars by pouring off extra into a cup
- **Educational Benefit**: recognize and draw star shapes (10 sides=decagon, corners=vertices [singular is vertex])
- **Optional Incentive**: enjoy star-shaped snacks, stay up past bedtime on a clear night to look at stars, hang some glow-in-the-dark stars on bedroom ceiling

Self-Control Remote

"Like a city whose walls are broken through
is a person who lacks self-control."
Proverbs 25:28

- **Goal**: self-control / peace
- **Preparation Time**: 5-10 minutes
- **Materials Needed**: copy of following page, crayons, scissors
- **How to Use**: Cut out a remote and write a self-control goal on top Have child color in each "button" when self-control is demonstrated.
- **Additional Ideas**: Purchase candy buttons to put on remote and allow child to eat one each time self-control is shown.
- **Hint**: use for chores or to earn t.v., computer, or video game privileges
- **Educational Benefit**: word and shape recognition
- **Optional Incentive**: let child choose a family movie, such as Veggie Tales' "Josh and the Big Wall", to watch together (child can control the remote)

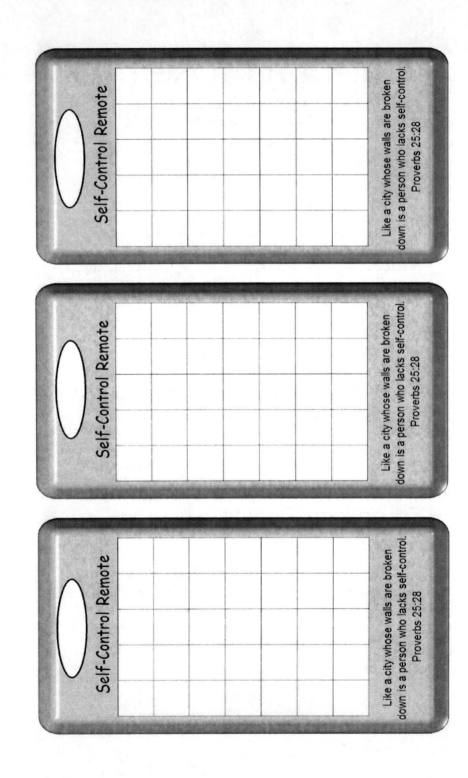

See Creatures

"We do not want you to become lazy,
but to imitate those who through faith and patience
inherit what has been promised."
Hebrews 6:12

- **Goal**: self-initiative / helpfulness
- **Preparation Time**: 0-5 minutes
- **Materials Needed**: blue paper, scissors, stickers of various sea creatures
- **How to Use**: Cut several small "waves" along blue paper. When child sees something that needs to be done and does it without being told (e.g. clearing table, dusting furniture, picking up siblings toys), place a sea creature sticker on a wave and label wave with accomplishment. Add more waves each time child takes initiative in doing something without being told.
- **Additional Ideas**: use as faith booster - when you "sea" God answer prayers, write it on sea creature, clip onto wave
- **Hint**: use pre-cut bulletin border (found in most craft or teacher stores) for waves
- **Educational Benefit**: recognizing sea creatures
- **Optional Incentive**: during bath time give small water capsules that dissolve into sea creature sponges (often found at dollar store), play "Go Fish"

Share Bear

"Share with the Lord's people who are in need.
Practice hospitality."
Romans 12:13

- **Goal**: thoughtfulness
- **Preparation Time**: 0-5 minutes
- **Materials Needed**: stuffed teddy bear (optional—name the bear "Share"), notebook, digital or Polaroid camera, printer, writing utensil, glue or tape
- **How to Use**: Each time sharing is demonstrated, take a picture of child holding Share, attach it to the top of a page in the Share Bear Journal, and have child write a sentence or two about what he/she did to demonstrate sharing and why.
- **Additional Ideas**: for younger children, let child be the "owner" of the Share Bear for a certain amount of time whenever child has demonstrated sharing
- **Hint**: when having difficulty sharing, read over journal together (make sure to date each entry)
- **Educational Benefit**: photography, journaling/writing
- **Optional Incentive**: bake some cupcakes with child and share with some friends or have some friends over to share child's toys

Sibling Revelry

"How good and pleasant it is when brothers [and sisters] dwell in unity!"
Psalm 133:1 (ESV)

- **Goal**: cooperation / encouragement
- **Preparation Time**: 0-5 minutes
- **Materials Needed**: photo of siblings together, plain cardstock or picture frame, scissors, glue or tape
- **How to Use**: Cut photo apart like a puzzle. Each time siblings demonstrate cooperation, encouragement or praise toward one another, give one piece of photo, until picture puzzle is complete.
- **Additional Ideas**: Each time siblings demonstrate cooperation or encouragement toward one another, tape one length of streamer in designated doorway (e.g. bedroom or hallway). Goal is to have streamers all the way across the door.
- **Hint**: This Booster is intended for at least two children who are old enough to verbally communicate feelings and comprehend the meaning of cooperation
- **Educational Benefit**: logic, spatial orientation
- **Optional Incentive**: time siblings completing a puzzle individually, then encourage them to work together cooperatively to see if they can beat their original time

Sign Me Up

"When he…saw what the grace of God had done, he was glad and encouraged them all to remain true to the Lord with all their hearts."
Acts 11:23

- **Goal**: behavior (righteousness)
- **Preparation Time**: 10-20 minutes
- **Materials Needed**: copies of various road signs, magnets, glue, writing utensil
- **How to Use**: Show your child(ren) the various traffic signs and discuss their meanings. Attach each sign to a magnet and place on fridge (or cookie sheet) at appropriate times (e.g. yield for when it's time to listen, stop for when it's time to obey, green light for free time, u-turn for come back and try again, etc.
- **Additional Ideas**: for multiple children print road signs on one page, write each child's name on a sticky note and put the sticky note on the appropriate sign for that child
- **Hint**: laminate signs or glue on cardboard for durability
- **Educational Benefit**: recognizing shapes, sight words, sign meanings
- **Optional Incentive**: when driving, point out signs and have child tell you what they represent

Smack!

"An honest answer is like a kiss on the lips."
Proverbs 24:26

- **Goal**: honesty
- **Preparation Time**: 0-5 minutes
- **Materials Needed**: mirror, thin tape or permanent marker, lipstick
- **How to Use**: Divide mirror into 8 (or other desired number) sections with marker or tape. Each time honesty is chosen, allow child to put on some lipstick and give the mirror a "smack" until all sections are filled.
- **Additional Ideas**: instead of mirror and lipstick, use divided paper and draw or glue on pictures of lips
- **Hint**: if there is concern about boys wearing lipstick, use chap stick instead
- **Educational Benefit**: counting, graphing
- **Optional Incentive**: wax lips and candy lipstick, anyone?

Smartie Pants

"The fear of the Lord is the beginning of knowledge, but fools despise wisdom and instruction."
Proverbs 1:7

- **Goal**: wise choices
- **Preparation Time**: 0-5 minutes
- **Materials Needed**: Smartie candies, cardboard, scissors, tube frosting, writing utensil
- **How to Use**: Cut a pair of pants from cardboard. Write Scripture across the top as a belt. Have child decorate the pants with Smarties, using frosting as glue. Each time a wise choice is made, child may eat a Smartie.
- **Additional Ideas**: use for general or specific behavior, chores done independently, good sportsmanship, completed homework, etc.
- **Hint**: make multiple pairs of pants if using for more than one child or more than one behavior
- **Educational Benefit**: art, science (frosting is soft, but dries hard)
- **Optional Incentive**: encourage friends to be "Smartie Pants"

Sneakers

"If I have walked with falsehood or my foot has hurried after deceit--let God weigh me in honest scales."
Job 31:5-6a

- **Goal**: honesty (eliminate sneakiness)
- **Preparation Time**: 0-5 minutes
- **Materials Needed**: sneaker that's not being used and a shoelace
- **How to Use**: Remove shoelace from sneaker. Each time child chooses to be honest instead of sneaky, thread shoelace through one hole. Continue to do so each time child chooses honesty over sneakiness (or dishonesty) until sneaker is completely threaded. Make a celebration out of tying the "completed" sneaker.
- **Additional Ideas**: Draw a sneaker out of an old shoebox lid, cut out, and punch holes to thread shoelace through or use a sneaker from when the child was smaller.
- **Hint**: for older children make more holes or one sneaker per area (e.g. eating when not allowed, taking money, calling a friend before doing homework)
- **Educational Benefit**: lacing, tying, fine motor skills
- **Optional Incentive**: get a new pair of shoes, have a foot race, go to a park to "test out" those sneakers

Son-Dial

"If anyone acknowledges that Jesus is the Son of God, God lives in them and they in God."
1 John 4:15

- **Goal**: attitude (honoring Jesus)
- **Preparation Time**: 5-10 minutes
- **Materials Needed**: large cardboard circle or paper plate, attachable spinner, 4-8 weather stickers or clip-art pictures (sunny, stormy, cloudy, lightning, tornado, rainy, etc.)
- **How to Use**: Divide the circle into equal sections with spinner in center. Spinner should stay in place when turned. 1st section–attach sun picture, 2nd section–cloudy, 3rd section–party cloudy, 4th section–stormy. Have child position spinner pointing to appropriate spot depending current attitude. Goal is to remain on sunny section with a bright, cheery attitude reflecting the Son. Pray with child when not on appropriate section to live as a child of God.
- **Additional Ideas**: rule of thumb: use 1 sticker per year of child's age, plus sun sticker
- **Hint**: use brad, paperclip, and paper plate instead of spinner and circle
- **Educational Benefit**: fractions, weather
- **Optional Incentive**: have a family picnic on a sunny day

Sonflower

"He…hears my words and puts them into practice."
Luke 6:47b

- **Goal**: self-initiative / thoughtfulness
- **Preparation Time**: 0-5 minutes
- **Materials Needed**: copy of following page, sunflower seeds, glue, yellow marker
- **How to Use**: Have child color the Sonflower petals yellow. Each time child is a *doer* and not just a *hearer* of God's Word, glue a seed onto the center of the flower until it is full.
- **Additional Ideas**: use when child demonstrates Christ-like behavior (Jesus Christ is God's Son)
- **Hint**: since seeds will weigh down the flower after a few are glued on, attach sunflower picture to cardboard
- **Educational Benefit**: counting, coloring
- **Optional Incentive**: pick or plant flowers together

Sonflower

Hear my words and put them into practice.
Luke 6:47b

Sondae

"Who is it that overcomes the world?
Only the one who believes that Jesus is the Son of God."
1 John 5:5

- **Goal**: confidence
- **Preparation Time**: 0-5 minutes (grocery run may be necessary)
- **Materials Needed**: ingredients to make an ice cream sundae (more for older children, fewer for younger children)
- **How to Use**: Each time child "overcomes the world" by showing confidence in Jesus (e.g. resisting peer pressure), child may choose one ingredient to set aside toward the completion of the "sondae" until all ingredients have been earned.
- **Additional Ideas**: print out a picture of a sundae and have child color in each section as goal is demonstrated
- **Hint**: use for any behavior goal
- **Educational Benefit**: reading (ingredients), science, math (measurement)
- **Optional Incentive**: have a build-your-own-sundae celebration

Specktacles

"Why do you look at the speck of sawdust in your brother's eye and pay no attention to the plank in your own eye?"
Luke 6:41

- **Goal**: responsibility (of actions)
- **Preparation Time**: 0-5 minutes
- **Materials Needed**: pair of unneeded glasses, sand paper, scissors, glue
- **How to Use**: Cut out 2 sandpaper shapes the same size as the glasses. Cut both shapes into several small pieces and glue onto glasses to cover them up. When responsibility of actions is demonstrated without an argument, allow child to remove a piece of the sandpaper from the spectacles (like dirty glasses being wiped clean little by little).
- **Additional Ideas**: color glasses with black vis-à-vis then wipe off little by little, or if glasses aren't available, cut two circles from some finished cardboard and tape together to form mock spectacles
- **Hint**: purchase a pair of reading or sunglasses from a dollar store
- **Educational Benefit**: synonyms—spectacles & glasses
- **Optional Incentive**: let child choose a fun new pair of sunglasses (be sure it has 100% UV protection)

Sow What?

"Peacemakers who sow in peace reap a harvest of righteousness."
James 3:18

- **Goal**: peace / cooperation
- **Preparation Time**: 0-5 minutes
- **Materials Needed**: copy of following page, blunt plastic needle and string, tape, writing utensil
- **How to Use**: Thread a long piece of string through the needle, tape to the back of one stalk and string through the first piece of wheat. Each time peace is demonstrated, write it on the line and have child sew through one section of wheat stalk.
- **Additional Ideas**: there are two stalks to use for multiple children or for more than one example of peace
- **Hint**: instead of using needles, color in each piece of wheat when peace is demonstrated or glue on dried wheat (found at craft stores)
- **Educational Benefit**: homophones (sew, sow)
- **Optional Incentive**: make some wheat bread and eat while warm

Step Right Up!

"Since we live by the Spirit,
let us keep in step with the Spirit."
Galatians 5:25

- **Goal**: behavior
- **Preparation Time**: 5-10 minutes
- **Materials Needed**: Lego's, permanent marker (can remove with nail polish or hairspray later)
- **How to Use**: Set behavior goal(s). Each time child demonstrates desired behavior, connect Lego's to form steps. Write one word from Galatians 5:25 on the front of each Lego (see illustration below).
- **Additional Ideas**: write each word on an index card and tape to actual steps one at a time as child demonstrates desired behavior
- **Hint**: use wafers and writable frosting in place of Lego's
- **Educational Benefit**: fine motor skills, counting, spelling/reading
- **Optional Incentive**: go to a playground and climb the steps up to the slide while repeating verse

Strike a Pose

"In your relationships with one another, have the same mindset as Christ Jesus."
Philippians 2:5

- **Goal**: attitude
- **Preparation Time**: 10-15 minutes
- **Materials Needed**: child, camera, clothespin, way to print pictures
- **How to Use**: Take pictures of child making several expressions (angry, joyful, loving, pouty, etc.), print them out, and display them. Move clothespin to appropriate attitude. Goal is to stay on one that would be the same as Christ Jesus.
- **Additional Ideas**: have child draw expressions around the rim of a paper plate and attach a brad to a paperclip as an arrow to point to appropriate attitude
- **Hint**: for multiple children, take various shots of each child, or take group shots and have individually labeled clothespins
- **Educational Benefit**: understanding emotions
- **Optional Incentive**: let child take some pictures and create a personal photo album

Sweet Treat

"Even a child is known by his actions
by whether his conduct is pure and right."
Proverbs 20:11

- **Goal**: increase positive behavior
- **Preparation Time**: 5-10 minutes
- **Materials Needed**: copy of following page, scissors, writing utensil
- **How to Use**: Write child's name and/or behavior goal across the top of the 1st cupcake and have child decorate and cut apart the 2nd one. Each time child demonstrates desired behavior, glue a colored cupcake part onto plain cupcake in order (cupcake, frosting, whipped cream, cherry) until the treat is complete.
- **Additional Ideas**: use both copies for helping or Scripture memory (write helping job or Scripture reference on 1st copy and child colors or glues 2nd copy on top when goal is accomplished)
- **Hint**: laminate and attach velcro in order to reuse
- **Educational Benefit**: pictorial order, fine motor skills
- **Optional Incentive**: bake cupcakes together to enjoy

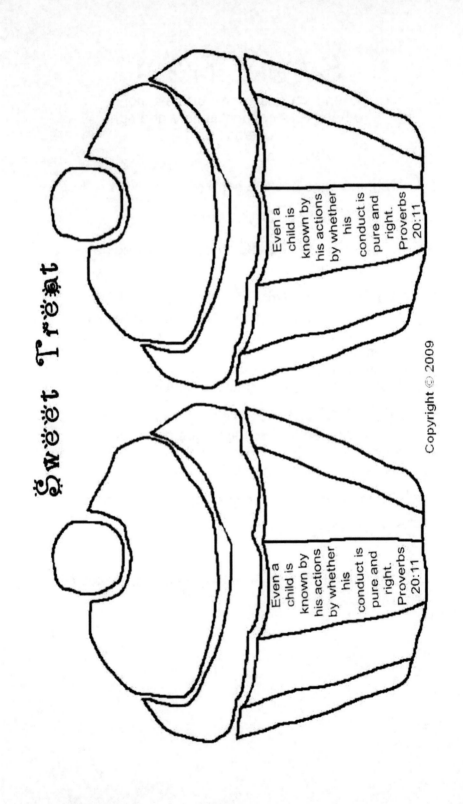

Sweet & Sour Children

"Do not grieve, for the joy of the Lord is your strength."
Nehemiah 8:10c

- **Goal**: attitude
- **Preparation Time**: 5-10 minutes
- **Materials Needed**: camera, way to print pictures, child(ren), glue
- **How to Use**: Take a picture of your child(ren) demonstrating a "sweet" face and a "sour" face. Print out, glue back to back, and post in a visible location (e.g. fridge). Flip photo to appropriate side depending on attitude.
- **Additional Ideas**: take a picture each time child has sweet attitude and post somewhere visible (don't post sour pictures—God's Word says to keep no record of wrongs)
- **Hint**: when child is struggling with attitude, re-read Nehemiah 8:10c and ask the Lord for strength to have joy
- **Educational Benefit**: photography, acting, opposites
- **Optional Incentive**: grab some Chinese take-out (be sure to order Sweet & Sour Chicken)

Tattle Tail

"Love does not delight in evil but rejoices with the truth."
1 Corinthians 13:6

- **Goal**: peace (reduce tattling)
- **Preparation Time**: 0-5 minutes
- **Materials Needed**: picture of a monkey (or another animal with a tail), brown pipe cleaners, scissors
- **How to Use**: Securely attach a pipe cleaner onto the monkey as a tail. Place somewhere visible. Curve the end of each pipe cleaner and attach to previous tail each time child resolves issue without tattling. If child tattles, remove a tail. Goal is reached when predetermined number of tails are hanging on the monkey.
- **Additional Ideas**: if tattling is not a problem, rename to "truth tail" or "monkey manners"…you get the idea…
- **Hint**: use the Barrel of Monkeys game to hang a monkey each time child chooses to solve problem without tattling
- **Educational Benefit**: counting, fine motor skills
- **Optional Incentive**: celebrate by eating some monkey bread or sharing a banana split

Taste Bud-dy

"Keep your tongue from evil and your lips from telling lies."
Psalm 34:13

- **Goal**: tone of voice / attitude
- **Preparation Time**: 0-5 minutes
- **Materials Needed**: copy of following page, black and pink crayons
- **How to Use**: Explain that the tongue has sweet and sour buds for *tasting*, but we often use our tongues to *speak* in a sweet or sour tone. Have child color a section of the tongue black when speaking "sour" and pink when speaking "sweet" until all sections of the Taste Bud-dy are filled. Discuss which color was used more (a black tongue looks awful!) and ways to continue improvement.
- **Additional Ideas**: Make two copies of Taste Bud-dy page and glue back to back. Color one tongue black (sour/bitter talk) and one tongue pink (sweet talk). Flip to appropriate side.
- **Hint**: laminate and use black and red vis-à-vis' in order to wash off and reuse
- **Educational Benefit**: parts of tongue, opposites
- **Optional Incentive**: lick a lollipop and taste its sweetness

Buddy

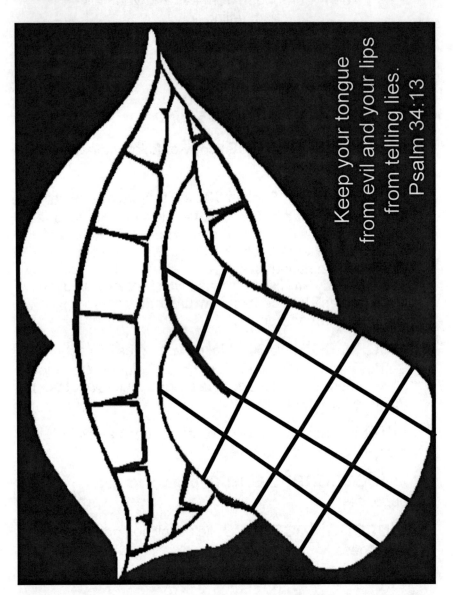

Keep your tongue from evil and your lips from telling lies.
Psalm 34:13

Taste

Ten Commandments Train

"My son, keep your father's commands and do not forsake your mother's teaching."
Proverbs 6:20

- **Goal**: obedience (following rules)
- **Preparation Time**: 5-10 minutes
- **Materials Needed**: 2 copies of following page, scissors, glue, writing utensil
- **How to Use**: Write a household rule in each train section on the 1st copy. Cut apart the 2nd copy. Each time a "commandment" is followed, glue the appropriate train piece onto 1st copy until train is complete.
- **Additional Ideas**: Cut apart ten rectangles to represent train cars. List one household commandment on each car. As child demonstrates, add car to the train.
- **Hint**: to simplify, make one copy of Ten Commandments Train page and child colors in each train part as goal is demonstrated
- **Educational Benefit**: ordinal numbers (1st train, 2nd train, etc.), pictorial skills (putting train pieces together), matching parts
- **Optional Incentive**: make a candy train – hot glue one roll of lifesavers to the top of a pack of gum for train body, 4 hard peppermints as wheels, chocolate kiss as funnel

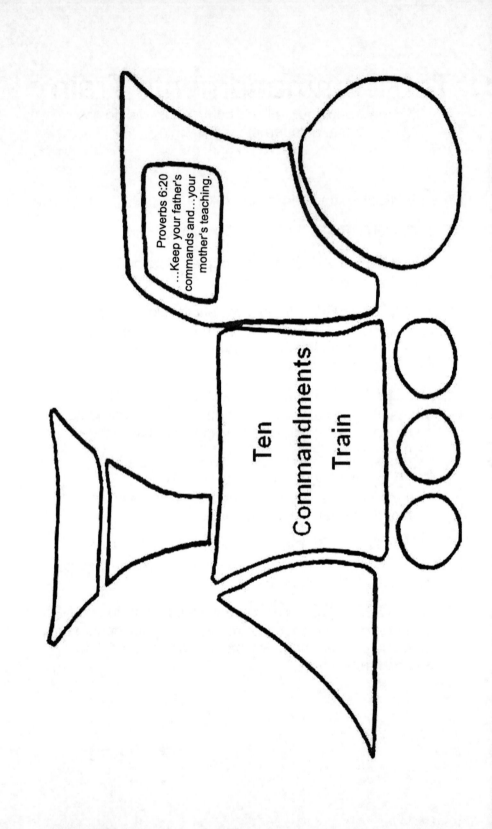

Terrific Tickets

"Love must be sincere.
Hate what is evil, cling to what is good."
Romans 12:9

- **Goal**: behavior
- **Preparation Time**: 5-10 minutes (extra time later for "store" [see How to Use])
- **Materials Needed**: carnival tickets (find at office supply store)
- **How to Use**: Set goals (1-2 goals x age) with child. Give 5 tickets at the start of each week, regardless of how many child has from previous weeks. When child is behaving (being terrific), give ticket. When not behaving, take ticket away. At the end of the week, child may "buy" pre-purchased items from your "store" (candy, dollar store items, doll, jewelry, train, eating out, etc.). Reuse tickets, or as child "spends" them, write good behavior on the back and review them at the beginning of the next week.
- **Additional Ideas**: When child leaves out toys/items or is arguing over them, place in "toy jail". If child needs items immediately (shoes, school book, etc.), charge 2 tickets. If child can wait, they must buy items out of jail before they can shop. If there are items they don't want to buy from toy jail, it's time to donate them.
- **Hint**: appropriate age would be 4 years and up
- **Educational Benefit**: earning, spending, saving

That's Twisted

"A cord of three strands is not quickly broken."
Ecclesiastes 4:12b

- **Goal**: trust
- **Preparation Time**: 0-5 minutes
- **Materials Needed**: licorice
- **How to Use**: Show child 3 strands of licorice. Demonstrate how easily one breaks when it's alone. Then twist all 3 together and show how now it is not easily broken. When child demonstrates trust (either trusting or being trustworthy), give one strand of licorice. Goal is to earn 3 strands to braid together in a set amount of time (e.g. 1/day, 3/week).
- **Additional Ideas**: determine a number of licorice strands to earn instead of a set amount of time
- **Hint**: keep licorice in baggie to prevent it from drying out
- **Educational Benefit**: fine motor skills
- **Optional Incentive**: have spaghetti for dinner and make some breadsticks, but slice the bread dough into thin strips first, then twist three strands together to form braid before baking

This Little Light of Mine

"Your eye is the lamp of your body. When your eyes are healthy, your whole body also is full of light. But when they are unhealthy, your body also is full of darkness. See to it, then, that the light within you is not darkness."
Luke 11:34-35

- **Goal**: attitude
- **Preparation Time**: 0-5 minutes
- **Materials Needed**: copy of following page, wiggly eyes
- **How to Use**: Each time child demonstrates goodness (with attitude or actions), put a wiggly eye on the lamp. If desired, black out eye with marker when negative behavior is shown. Goal is to cover the lamp with "good" eyes.
- **Additional Ideas**: cut out a light bulb and color one side yellow and one side black, then flip to appropriate side depending on attitude
- **Hint**: for multiple children, draw sunglasses around pairs of eyes when cooperation is demonstrated
- **Educational Benefit**: opposites (light & dark)
- **Optional Incentive**: have child choose a special night light for room to remind him that we should be "lights" for Jesus in a world of darkness (sin)

Truthful Tortoise

"Do not spread false reports."
Exodus 23:1a

- **Goal**: honesty
- **Preparation Time**: 0-5 minutes
- **Materials Needed**: copy of following page on green paper (if desired), stickers
- **How to Use**: Each time child demonstrates honesty, he/she may place a sticker on one section of the tortoise. By the time the tortoise shell is filled in, child should be in a positive habit of telling the truth.
- **Additional Ideas**: instead of stickers, color in each section or use tissue paper (like a mosaic)
- **Hint**: Remind children that lying (and gossiping) may *seem* fun, but the Bible tells us that we are to ALWAYS to tell the truth about everything and everyone.
- **Educational Benefit**: read <u>The Tortoise and the Hare</u>
- **Optional Incentive**: play "Hare, Hare, Tortoise" (same as Duck, Duck, Goose), except the Tortoise crawls and the Hare hops, laying down for a short nap half-way around the circle.

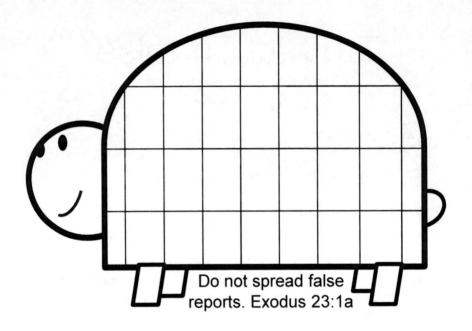

Truthful Tortoise

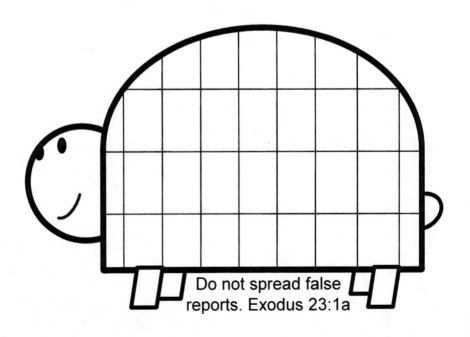

Truth Time

"Truthful lips endure forever, but a lying tongue lasts only a moment."
Proverbs 12:19

- **Goal**: honesty
- **Preparation Time**: 5-10 minutes
- **Materials Needed**: plate, number stickers 1-12 (or marker), spinner (or brad and paperclip)
- **How to Use**: Create a clock using the materials listed. Point spinner to "twelve o'clock". Each time child demonstrates honesty, go forward one "hour". When child demonstrates dishonesty, go back an "hour". Goal is to reach 12 in a timely manner.
- **Additional Ideas**: Cut out 12 strips of paper the length from the center of the plate to the number. Each time child demonstrates honesty, write it on strip and glue from center toward appropriate number to review and remember.
- **Hint**: For multiple children, use clothespins with child's name written on each one and clip to edge of plate beginning at 12. Move to next number when honesty is demonstrated.
- **Educational Benefit**: numbers 1-12, addition
- **Optional Incentive**: purchase a watch for child as a reminder that it is always the right time to tell the truth

V-I-C-T-O-R-Y

"May we shout for joy over your victory
and lift up our banners in the name of our God."
Psalm 20:5

- **Goal**: joyfulness
- **Preparation Time**: 0-5 minutes
- **Materials Needed**: seven ½-¼ sheets of construction paper, thick marker, yarn, hole punch, tape
- **How to Use**: Punch a hole in the top two corners of each piece of paper. Write one letter of VICTORY on each sheet. Each time joyfulness is demonstrated, string a letter onto the yarn (displayed in visible location) until the VICTORY banner is complete and child is victorious.
- **Additional Ideas**: for general behavior have 7 blank post-it notes on display and have child write a letter each time positive behavior is demonstrated
- **Hint**: for multiple children spell out each child's name to completion (don't make it a competition—there will probably be a different number of letters in each name)
- **Educational Benefit**: spelling, fine motor skills
- **Optional Incentive**: go to a local high school sports game and cheer them on toward victory

Waves of Mercy

"He saved us, not because of righteous things we had done, but because of His mercy."

Titus 3:5a

- **Goal**: attitude (mercy [a disposition to be kind and forgiving])
- **Preparation Time**: 5-10 minutes
- **Materials Needed**: copy of following page, scissors, blue paper, tape or sticky tac
- **How to Use**: While child is decorating the Mercy boat, cut the blue paper into wavy strips. Cover boat entirely with waves. Remove a wave each time child demonstrates mercy until waves are all gone and only the colorful Mercy Boat remains.
- **Additional Ideas**: write examples of mercy on each wave and remove wave when child shows that particular example of mercy
- **Hint**: use real boat for a 3-D effect and tape waves onto it, covering the entire boat
- **Educational Benefit**: subtraction of parts to reveal hidden item
- **Optional Incentive**: take a boat ride to feel the rocking of waves or play with some toy boats in the pool and make them "sail" over waves

Waves of Mercy

"He saved us, not because of righteous things we had done, but because of His mercy."
Titus 3:5a

A Whale of a Lesson

"O Lord, I knew that you are a <u>gracious</u> and <u>compassionate</u> God, <u>slow to anger</u> and <u>abounding in love</u>; a God who <u>relents from sending calamity</u>."
Jonah 4:2b

- **Goal**: Scripture application
- **Preparation Time**: 0-5 minutes
- **Materials Needed**: copy of following page, crayons
- **How to Use**: Read Jonah 4:2b and explain the meaning of each underlined section. As child demonstrates under-standing and application of the phrases listed, color in appropriate section on the whale's spout.
- **Additional Ideas**: use the same way, but change the five phrases to other applicable lessons for your child(ren)
- **Hint**: use as a team or make one copy for each child
- **Educational Benefit**: vocabulary
- **Optional Incentive**: watch the Veggie Tales movie "Jonah" for a fun family movie

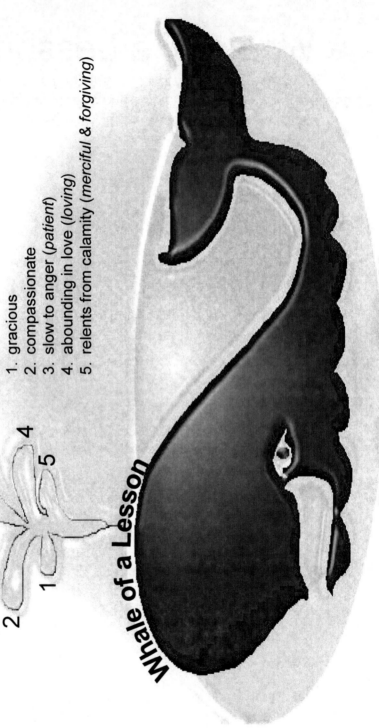

Jonah 4:2b Characteristics:
1. gracious
2. compassionate
3. slow to anger (*patient*)
4. abounding in love (*loving*)
5. relents from calamity (*merciful & forgiving*)

Whale of a Lesson

Wheel of Blessings

"Enter his gates with thanksgiving and his courts with praise; give thanks to him and praise his name."
Psalm 100:4

- **Goal**: behavior
- **Preparation Time**: 5-10 minutes
- **Materials Needed**: 2 paper plates (or large circles), brad, scissors, writing utensil
- **How to Use**: Draw 5-8 rectangles on the 2nd paper plate. Write a goal (see Hint) in each rectangle. On the 1st plate, cut out one rectangle the same size and location. Attach plates with the brad directly in the center (optional). Have child turn the wheel daily (or until goal is mastered) and work on whichever goal appears.
- **Additional Ideas**: For multiple children write each child's name in a rectangle, goal behavior on the top plate and have the child whose name appears through the cut-out be the one to praise the other children working on that goal.
- **Hint**: use for behavior, chores, helping, ways to show kindness or respect, Scripture memory, etc.
- **Educational Benefit**: reading, assembling, rectangles
- **Optional Incentive**: watch Wheel of Fortune together

Why Knot?

"By faith Abraham…obeyed and went, even though he did not know where he was going."
Hebrews 11:8

- **Goal**: obedience
- **Preparation Time**: 0-5 minutes
- **Materials Needed**: thin rope or thick yarn, candies or other small "rewards" (optional)
- **How to Use**: Just as Abraham did not ask why, but simply had faith and obeyed, it is important that a child obey without delay. Tie several loose knots in a rope, spaced apart (1-2 knots per age of child). Child may untie a knot when obedience without delaying or arguing is demonstrated.
- **Additional Ideas**: put something small in each knot that child may keep when untying (e.g. dime, small candy, sticker).
- **Hint**: for older children, research all the different types of knots and challenge child to tie particular ones the night before to prepare for the next day
- **Educational Benefit**: fine motor skills, knot names and familiarity
- **Optional Incentive**: go to a sports shop or gym and climb a rope ladder

Wise as an Owl

"Woe to those who are wise in their own eyes
and clever in their own sight."
Isaiah 5:21

- **Goal**: humility
- **Preparation Time**: 5-10 minutes
- **Materials Needed**: brown or speckled feathers (from craft store), large picture of owl (find online or in an animal coloring book), glue
- **How to Use**: Humility is always a wise decision. Each time humility is demonstrated, allow child to glue a feather onto the owl.
- **Additional Ideas**: Write examples of humility on several owls. When child demonstrates that example, glue a feather on that particular owl.
- **Hint**: have child design a large owl for which to glue on feathers
- **Educational Benefit**: art, science (explore owls)
- **Optional Incentive**: visit a bird sanctuary and view many of God's colorfully feathered birds

Wisdom Rock

"Everyone who hears these words of mine and
puts them into practice is like a wise man
who built his house on the rock."
Matthew 7:24

- **Goal**: wise choices
- **Preparation Time**: 5-10 minutes
- **Materials Needed**: large rock, marker or paint
- **How to Use**: Clean the rock. Write W I S D O M across rock (leave space around each letter). Each time child puts God's Word into practice by making wise choices, draw a house around one of the letters on the rock.
- **Additional Ideas**: Start with a plain rock, then add a letter each time child makes a wise choices until the word "WISDOM" is complete.
- **Hint**: use thin electrical tape to make houses in order to remove "houses" and reuse rock
- **Educational Benefit**: spelling
- **Optional Incentive**: make a sandcastle at the playground and pour water on top to observe how it dissolves, then pour water over a rock and note that it remains solid (much like our choices with or without God)

X-Ray Vision

"The Lord does not look at the things people look at. People look at the outward appearance, but the Lord looks at the heart."
1 Samuel 16:7b

- **Goal**: attitude
- **Preparation Time**: 0-5 minutes
- **Materials Needed**: heart (cut from cardboard, or a toy), plastic wrap
- **How to Use**: Write the above verse on the heart. Cut 24-25 sheets of plastic wrap (1 for each word in 1 Samuel 16:7b) large enough to cover the front and have child layer the heart. Each time child demonstrates a caring attitude toward someone, unwrap one sheet. Goal is to completely reveal the heart; seeing it clearly and not being distracted by what was covering it on the outside.
- **Additional Ideas**: write one word of 1 Samuel 16:7b above on each layer of wrap and review verse each time child removes a sheet
- **Hint**: for younger children use fewer sheets and group words from the verse together
- **Educational Benefit**: reading, prediction
- **Optional Incentive**: volunteer to serve a meal at a homeless shelter and get to know the *inside* of people; not their outward *appearance*

Yes I Can! Can

"I can do all things through him who gives me strength."
Philippians 4:13

- **Goal**: confidence / attitude
- **Preparation Time**: 5-10 minutes
- **Materials Needed**: clean can (or see Hint), wrapping paper, tape, writing utensil, small slips of paper
- **How to Use**: Wrap can and entitle "Yes I Can!". Write things child can do on slips of paper and put in can (e.g. You can make your bed without any help. You can say the Lord's Prayer. You can help Mom pour the milk. You can help Dad take out the trash). When child is discouraged, read some of the can-do's.
- **Additional Ideas**: use for homework, sports, chores, Scripture memory, etc.
- **Hint**: use Crystal Light container instead of metal can for safety and cleanliness
- **Educational Benefit**: reading, writing
- **Optional Incentive**: let child take time to show parent how to do something (follow a recipe, put in a movie, hit the baseball)

Yield

"…yield your hearts to the Lord…"
Joshua 24:23b

- **Goal**: obedience
- **Preparation Time**: 5-10 minutes
- **Materials Needed**: red triangles, white hearts, sticky tac, glue
- **How to Use**: Post predetermined number of triangles (point down) on wall. Each time child chooses to yield to instruction (obey), write it on the heart and glue onto triangle.
- **Additional Ideas**: write one letter of "yield" onto each heart before gluing to triangle
- **Hint**: read further into Joshua about the struggles the Israelites had trusting and obeying God, yet when they yielded their hearts to the Lord, He provided for their needs and gave them abundantly more than they asked for
- **Educational Benefit**: shapes, spelling, vocabulary
- **Optional Incentive**: take a drive and count how many yield signs, then discuss why it's important to yield at those spots

Zip It

"Glorify the Lord with me; let us exalt His name together."
Psalm 34:3

- **Goal**: tone of voice
- **Preparation Time**: 0-5 minutes
- **Materials Needed**: old knit glove, zipper, craft or fabric glue, wiggly eyes (optional)
- **How to Use**: Have child create a face on the glove, gluing the zipper sideways where a mouth should be. When the puppet "mouth" is open/unzipped, child is free to talk. However, each time mouth is used unkindly, have child zip the mouth shut on the puppet, as well as their own for as many minutes as their age.
- **Additional Ideas**: start with zipper open and make marks every ½ inch apart, then move zipper in appropriate direction depending on tone of voice
- **Hint**: zippers can be found at most fabric stores or remove one from clothing that isn't worn anymore
- **Educational Benefit**: opposites (open/close), art
- **Optional Incentive**: let child choose outfit the next day

Topical Index
Behavior

A"maize"ing Grace	attitude
aCROSStic	attitude
Attitude Adjustors	attitude
Clean Heart	attitude
Crown Him with Many Crayons	attitude
Grate-fullness	attitude
GRRRattitude	attitude
Hide & Seek-Ye-First	attitude
Mouth Trap	attitude
No Whine Vine, The	attitude
Son Dial	attitude
Strike a Pose	attitude
Sweet & Sour Children	attitude
Taste Bud-dy	attitude
This Little Light of Mine	attitude
Waves of Mercy	attitude
X-Ray Vision	attitude
Yes I Can! Can	attitude
Behavior Beans	behavior
Behavior Bucks	behavior
Caterpillar Countdown	behavior
Cookie Jar	behavior
Cookie Press	behavior
Cross Stitch	behavior
God's Handy-work	behavior
God's Team	behavior
Grow Up	behavior
Heavenly Pair-a-Dice	behavior
Map Quest	behavior
Marbleous Jar	behavior
Master Blaster	behavior
Muscle Man	behavior
Opossum Opposites	behavior
Rainbow of _____	behavior
Red Light, Green Light	behavior
Sign Me Up	behavior
Smartie Pants	behavior

Step Right Up	behavior
Sweet Treat	behavior
Terrific Tickets	behavior
Wheel of Blessings	behavior
Bloomin' Onion	confidence
Boldness Baldy	confidence
Fearless Freddy	confidence
I Am Cape-Able	confidence
Yes I Can! Can	confidence
Arky, Arky	cooperation
Cooperation Coordinates	cooperation
Har-money	cooperation
Sibling Revelry	cooperation
Sow What?	cooperation
That's Twisted!	cooperation
Building Blocks	encouragement
Catch Praise	encouragement
Encouragement Elephant	encouragement
In Today's News…	encouragement
Sibling Revelry	encouragement
Fix-It Shop	forgiveness
Hairy Helper	helpfulness
Hamburger Helper	helpfulness
Helping Hippo	helpfulness
See Creatures	helpfulness
Delite Bright	honesty
Put a Cork in It	honesty
Smack!	honesty
Sneakers	honesty
Truth Time	honesty
Truthful Tortoise	honesty
Humble Pie	humility
Wise as an Owl	humility
Cheery O's	joyfulness
Fill 'er Up	joyfulness
Glad-Libs	joyfulness
Happiness Hippo	joyfulness
J-O-Y Full	joyfulness
Joyful Jumping Jack	joyfulness
Keep me in Stitches	joyfulness
Music Machine	joyfulness

V-I-C-T-O-R-Y	joyfulness
Butterfly Kisses	kindness
Caring Caterpillar	kindness
Caring Clover	kindness
Friendship Fish	kindness
Honey, Honey	kindness
Kinder Reminder	kindness
Money Talks	kindness
Butterfly Kisses	love
Caring Caterpillar	love
Caring Clover	love
Chocolate Lovers	love
Kinder Reminder	love
Love Links	love
Love One AnUdder	love
Love Reporter	love
Power of Love	love
Eggs-actly!	obedience
Hot Stuff	obedience
Red Hot Obedience Pot	obedience
Respecter Gadget	obedience
Ruler of All	obedience
Ten Commandments Train	obedience
Why Knot?	obedience
Yield	obedience
Last Place	patience
Listening *Lips*	patience
Patient Prince(ss)	patience
Quick Sand	patience
Complaint Can	peace
Do-Unto's	peace
Dream Weaver	peace
Frustration Station	peace
Puzzle Peace	peace
Self-Control Remote	peace
Sow What?	peace
Tattle Tail	peace
I Refuze	peer pressure
Sondae	peer pressure
Call Me	prayer
Flower Power	prayer

Friends Fries	prayer
Picture Prayers	prayer
Popcorn Praise	prayer
Manner Marks	respect
Respecter Gadget	respect
Chore Champ	responsibility
Responsibility Chart	responsibility
Specktacles	responsibility
Advent-ures	Scripture application
Attitude Adjustors	Scripture application
Bee Attitudes	Scripture application
Dress-a-Bear	Scripture application
Fearless Freddy	Scripture application
Fruit of the Spirit Tree	Scripture application
Home Sweet Home	Scripture application
Knight in Shining Armor	Scripture application
Love Links	Scripture application
Pure Nonsense	Scripture application
Whale of a Lesson, A	Scripture application
Button Basket	self-control
Do-Unto's	self-control
Self-Control Remote	self-control
Ants in My Pants	self-initiative
Doer Daisy	self-initiative
Get Up!	self-initiative
Maker's Doesen	self-initiative
See Creatures	self-initiative
Sonflower	self-initiative
Be the 1	thankfulness
Bless You Box	thankfulness
Bountiful Blessings	thankfulness
God Rocks!	thankfulness
Grate-fullness	thankfulness
GRRRattitude	thankfulness
Doer Daisy	thoughtfulness
Hmmm…Interesting	thoughtfulness
Last Place	thoughtfulness
M&M's	thoughtfulness
Maker's Doesen	thoughtfulness
Salt & Light	thoughtfulness
Share Bear	thoughtfulness

Sonflower	thoughtfulness
Button Basket	tone of voice
Money Talks	tone of voice
Mouth Trap	tone of voice
No Whine Vine, The	tone of voice
Penny for Your Talks	tone of voice
Taste Bud-dy	tone of voice
Zip It	tone of voice
Color by Number	wise choices
Faithful "Fall"ower	wise choices
Fisher of Men	wise choices
Heart of Wisdom	wise choices
Ought-to-Dot	wise choices
Pearly Gates	wise choices
Wisdom Rock	wise choices

Topical Index
Scripture

Cross Stitch	1 Corinthians 1:18
Building Blocks	1 Corinthians 8:1b
Boldness Baldy	1 Corinthians 10:31b
Hairy Helper	1 Corinthians 10:31b
Caring Clover	1 Corinthians 12:24-25
Love Links	1 Corinthians 13:4-8a
Tattle Tail	1 Corinthians 13:6
Cookie Jar	1 John 2:17
Love One AnUdder	1 John 4:7a
Love Reporter	1 John 4:11
Son-Dial	1 John 4:15
Power of Love	1 John 4:21
Sondae	1 John 5:5
Manner Marks	1 Peter 2:17
Attitude Adjustors	1 Peter 3:8
X-Ray Vision	1 Samuel 16:7b
Encouragement Elephant	1 Thessalonians 5:11a
Puzzle Peace	1 Thessalonians 5:13
Patient Prince(ss)	1 Thessalonians 5:14b
Behavior Bucks	1 Thessalonians 5:15
Kinder Reminder	1 Thessalonians 5:15b
Marbleous Jar	1 Timothy 4:12
Caring Caterpillar	1 Timothy 5:4
Fearless Freddy	2 Timothy 1:7
Grow Up	2 Peter 3:18a
Caterpillar Countdown	3 John 1:11
Sign Me Up	Acts 11:23
Bless You Box	Acts 20:35b
aCROSStic	Colossians 3:2
Put a Cork in It	Colossians 3:9a
Dress-a-Bear	Colossians 3:12
GRRRattitude	Colossians 3:16
Eggs-actly!	Colossians 3:20
Flower Power	Colossians 4:2
Hot Stuff	Daniel 3
Arky, Arky	Ecclesiastes 4:9
That's Twisted!	Ecclesiastes 4:12b

Dream Weaver	Ecclesiastes 5:3
A"maize"ing Grace	Ephesians 2:8a
Red Hot Obedience Pot	Ephesians 6:1
Knight in Shining Armor	Ephesians 6:11
Button Basket	Exodus 4:12
Truthful Tortoise	Exodus 23:1a
I Refuze	Exodus 23:2a
Fruit of the Spirit Tree	Galatians 5:22-23
Step Right Up	Galatians 5:25
Rainbow of _____	Genesis 9:13
Pearly Gates	Genesis 28:17
In Today's News…	Hebrews 3:13
See Creatures	Hebrews 6:12
Why Knot?	Hebrews 11:8
Wise as an Owl	Isaiah 5:21
Complaint Can	Isaiah 29:24b
J-O-Y Full	Isaiah 61:10a
Listening *Lips*	James 1:19
Doer Daisy	James 1:22
Sow What?	James 3:18
Ought-to-Dot	James 4:17
Happiness Hippo	James 5:13b
Picture Prayers	James 5:16a
Bloomin' Onion	Jeremiah 17:17
Butterfly Kisses	Jeremiah 31:3
Friends Fries	Job 16:21
Sneakers	Job 31:5-6a
No-Whine Vine, The	John 15:5
Whale of a Lesson, A	Jonah 4:2b
Yield	Joshua 24:23b
Advent-ures	Luke 2
Do-Unto's	Luke 6:31
Specktacles	Luke 6:41
Sonflower	Luke 6:47b
Behavior Beans	Luke 11:28
This Little Light of Mine	Luke 11:34-35
Be the 1	Luke 17:11-19
God Rocks!	Luke 19:40
Fisher of Men	Matthew 4:19-20
Salt & Light	Matthew 5:13-16
Bee Attitudes	Matthew 5:3-11

Fix-It Shop	Matthew 6:14
Master Blaster	Matthew 6:24
Hide & Seek-Ye-First	Matthew 6:33
Wisdom Rock	Matthew 7:24
Last Place	Matthew 20:16
Sweet & Sour Children	Nehemiah 8:10c
Hmmm…Interesting	Philippians 2:4
Strike a Pose	Philippians 2:5
Grate-fullness	Philippians 2:14
Cookie Press	Philippians 3:12b
Chore Champ	Philippians 3:14
Yes I Can! Can	Philippians 4:13
Pure Nonsense	Philippians 4:8
Smartie Pants	Proverbs 1:7
Hamburger Helper	Proverbs 3:27
Faithful "Fall"ower	Proverbs 3:3a
Helping Hippo	Proverbs 4:20
Ten Commandments Train	Proverbs 6:20
Ants in My Pants	Proverbs 6:6
Humble Pie	Proverbs 11:2
Mouth Trap	Proverbs 12:13
Truth Time	Proverbs 12:19
Delite Bright	Proverbs 12:22
Respecter Gadget	Proverbs 13:13
Responsibility Chart	Proverbs 14:22b
Quick Sand	Proverbs 14:29
Cheery O's	Proverbs 15:13
God's Team	Proverbs 15:18
Honey, Honey	Proverbs 16:24
Friendship Fish	Proverbs 17:17a
Joyful Jumping Jack	Proverbs 17:22
Maker's Doesen	Proverbs 20:11
Money Talks	Proverbs 22:11
Sweet Treat	Proverbs 22:11
Home Sweet Home	Proverbs 24:3-4
Smack!	Proverbs 24:26
Self-Control Remote	Proverbs 25:28
Glad-Libs	Psalm 16:9
Muscle Man	Psalm 18:32
God's Handy-work	Psalm 19:1
V-I-C-T-O-R-Y	Psalm 20:5a

Get Up!	Psalm 20:8b
Crown Him with Many Crayons	Psalm 24:10
Zip It	Psalm 34:3
Taste Bud-dy	Psalm 34:13
I am Cape-Able	Psalm 46:1
Red Light, Green Light	Psalm 46:1
Clean Heart	Psalm 51:7b
Heart of Wisdom	Psalm 90:12
Color by Number	Psalm 90:12
Music Machine	Psalm 100:1
Wheel of Blessings	Psalm 100:4
Bountiful Blessings	Psalm 118:1
Opossum Opposites	Psalm 119:9
Chocolate Lovers	Psalm 119:11
Ruler of All	Psalm 119:133
Keep Me in Stitches	Psalm 126:2a
Sibling Revelry	Psalm 133:1
Penny for Your Talks	Psalm 139:4
Map Quest	Psalm 139:23-24
Call Me	Psalm 145:18
Popcorn Praise	Psalm 147:1
Heavenly Pair-a-Dice	Romans 8:8-9a
Terrific Tickets	Romans 12:9
Catch Praise	Romans 12:10
Share Bear	Romans 12:13
Har-money	Romans 12:16a
Cooperation Coordinates	Romans 12:16
M&M's	Romans 14:19
Frustration Station	Romans 15:4
Fill 'er Up	Romans 15:13
Waves of Mercy	Titus 3:5

CPSIA information can be obtained at www.ICGtesting.com
Printed in the USA
LVOW12s0751310813

350080LV00006B/14/P